What they're saying about *Don't Quit Five Minutes Before the Miracle Happens*

In *Don't Quit Five Minutes Before the Miracle Happens*, Jeannie strikes an impressive balance of boldness and vulnerability, authenticity and candor, and somberness and celebration that will leave you laughing in hysteria one moment and crying on your sleeve the next. In the way only Jeannie can, she takes you on the roller coaster of her life with a refreshing rawness that is extraordinarily genuine. You will find it difficult to put this book down as she discusses her own history of childhood abuse, addiction, rape, financial ruin, and more of life's most challenging traumas. She gives you the details of her life story and then explains how God saved her from her abusers—at times the most significant being herself.

Through this book Jeannie points us to Jesus in a way that is simple yet so very profound. She discusses how she began healing under His direction with practical truths the reader can not only grasp, but replicate. Jeannie leads by example as she has faithfully and diligently worked through layers of trauma that the enemy meant for her destruction. As I read these pages, I could literally see Jesus, saying to Jeannie, "No, Satan. That one is mine. I have bought and paid for her with my life, and I will do it again and again. Take your hands off my child!" Jeannie's story is one of celebration and triumph. She is a beautiful example of God's promise to work all things for the good of those who love Him. Allow Jeannie to take you through her life as she learned to trade in her victimhood for victory in Jesus.

"And we know that in all things God works for the good of those who love him, who have been called according to his purpose." (Romans 8:28)

"Consider it pure joy ... whenever you face trials of many kinds, because you know that the testing of your faith develops perseverance." (James 1:2-3)

Dr. Jana Lovelace

Licensed clinical psychologist and co-founder of No Limits Women's Conferences, LLC, Decatur, AL

When I first started reading this book, I vividly followed the life of several of my former students. Jeannie's life mirrored those hurt souls I encountered over my 25-year educational career. However, the epiphany came as I delved into the later chapters and saw similarities to my own life. I have to be the strong one for everyone. I'm an overachiever whose pride can get in the way of health issues. Wow! It's so amazing the way God allows others to be a vessel in our lives. I recommend this book to anyone looking for "real talk" and a soul-searching journey.

Dr. Andrain Y. Jones

Educator, Harvest, AL

As Christians, we believe the Good News is good news because the reality of sin in our lives separates us from a holy and perfect God. Christ's death and resurrection reconcile us with God, and in His mercy we are being healed and made new. Jeannie's willingness to be vulnerable and truthful about the hardships and struggles in her life magnifies and underscores the greatness and goodness of our God. In doing so, this book reminds us that saving faith is not a badge of superiority—rather, it is a free gift to broken sinners who receive it undeservedly. As a result, the book prompts a sense of humility about our own hopeless condition apart from Christ, deeper compassion for others, and more gratitude for our all-loving, all-powerful God who deeply wants a personal relationship with us.

John Joseph IV, JD

Executive Director, Startup Business Incubator, Decatur, AL

My heart has been so touched by Jeannie's story/ journey/testimony. My faith has been strengthened in so many ways. Never have I felt God's goodness, grace, mercy, love, and forgiveness like I do now after reading this book.

Karen Knight

Prayer Partner, Cullman, AL

I am honored to recommend, Don't Quit Five Minutes Before the Miracle Happens. Her story, like her life, is an inspiration to anyone seeking to escape an embattled past. She is an overcomer, finding strength and courage through Jesus Christ her Savior. She is a survivor, pursuing her calling and passion to help others find their purpose in life. I have been a witness to the power of God transforming her from the inside out. She didn't quit. She is tangible evidence of the miracle only God can bring.

Dawn Mason

Dawn Mason Ministries, Hartselle, AL

Don't Quit Five Minutes Before the Miracle Happens

Jeannie Lynch

A Servant's Heart
with Jeannie Lynch

Don't Quit Five Minutes Before the Miracle Happens
by Jeannie Lynch
© 2021 by Jeannie Lynch. All rights reserved.

Editing by Adam Colwell's WriteWorks, LLC, Adam Colwell and Ginger Colwell
Cover and logo design by Jimmy Anaya
Typesetting by Inktobook.com
Published by Adam Colwell's WriteWorks, LLC

Printed in the United States of America
ISBN (Paperback): 978-1-7356969-6-6
ISBN (eBook): 978-1-7356969-7-3

Dedication

This book is dedicated to God—who I truly believe opened up the gates of hell and let me out. His unconditional grace and mercy in healing this broken, crushed-in-spirit sinner is a story of redemption and renewal that only God could do.

The purpose of this book is for the words to touch the heart of the reader to move from darkness into the light—and to provide hope that if God can do it for me, He can absolutely do it for YOU!

I will serve you, God, all the days of my life. Use me up, Lord!

Table of Contents

Foreword

Donna Sparks

*Evangelist, author, and founder of Story of Grace
Prison Ministry*

When I first met Jeannie Lynch, I was absolutely clueless about the story that burned inside her. I knew she was a strong and gifted leader, but I was yet to learn about the pain and agony that forged the powerful woman she is.

Jeannie's testimony is raw and unfiltered. She shares her story with vivid, graphic, and heart-rending details. With total transparency, Jeannie brings us in close for a glimpse of a young, wounded heart searching for love and purpose.

As I read the twists and turns of her experiences, I often had to stop and marvel at all she survived and lived to tell about. The evidence of God's protection and loving care is visible on each and every page of her book.

The enemy of our souls wants to steal, kill, and destroy us. His evil influences are unmistakable and revealed in Jeannie's story, but she is an overcomer through Jesus Christ. In a gentle, loving way, it's clear that our Lord was often standing silently nearby Jeannie during all her experiences—her patient caretaker watching and waiting to come to her rescue.

But God's love wasn't evident only in protecting her. As God continued to work in her life, He also led her onto paths He specifically chose for her to walk on as He prepared her for the future. He brought not only salvation, healing, and deliverance but also purpose to a soul many would have considered a lost cause.

Step by step, Jeannie progressed in the faith. God gave her a brand new identity and a life filled with possibilities. The Lord gave her a loving church family to challenge her, disciple her, and help her grow in her relationship with Him. He blessed Jeannie, provided for her, and positioned her for amazing things!

Don't Quit Five Minutes Before the Miracle Happens will encourage you as it reveals how God reaches down and rescues those we might consider beyond reach. We may never be able to completely fathom the depths of God's love and mercy. But Jeannie's story provides to us living proof of it!

Acknowledgements

First and foremost, I want to acknowledge Jesus as my Lord and Savior. There are absolutely NO LIMITS with God. God led me through this entire process. Even though there were times when I did not desire to be as vulnerable as He wanted me to be, He guided me forward. He provided the strength and courage for this work. All the glory is His!

To my best friend and sister in Christ, Jana Lovelace. She literally held my hand through this entire process. Jana supported and pushed me. Every week she provided edits for that week's work. I prayed for years to have a friend like Jana. God blessed me far beyond what I had prayed for. Jana was the hands and feet of Jesus teaching me about trust.

To my church and pastors who spoke life over me and led me to Christ. I thank them for the lessons taught that led to the foundation for who I am in Christ and for the leadership class that refined me as a leader and helped prepare me to carry the mantle.

To my dear friend and sister in Christ, Angela Morgan, for sharing her talent and gifting of Scripture. God surely knew what He was doing when He crossed our paths.

To my editor, Adam Colwell. His faith, talent, and support cannot be measured.

To the team of prayer warriors who prayed for God's will and for me to be obedient to His will, and for the individuals who will read this book and be touched by the words to prompt them to turn toward Him and deepen their relationship with Him.

Finally, to everyone who has crossed my path in this life. To those who taught me through pain. Thank you. To those who were difficult to love and forgive. Thank you. To those who have loved and supported me. Thank you. To those very people who taught me not to trust and then those that did. Thank you. To those who have been a blessing to me and those who allowed me to be a blessing to them. Thank you.

Note from the Author

*M*y theme song is "I Am No Victim" by Kristene DiMarco—and just as its lyrics are all about who we are in Christ, it is my hope that this book will cause you to want to know everything about who *you* are in Jesus!

* * *

All profits from the sales of this book will go directly to the ministry of No Limits Women's Conferences, LLC.

ABOUT NO LIMIT'S WOMEN'S CONFERENCES, LLC

No Limits is a yearly conference that was born from the

hearts of Jeannie Lynch and Jana Lovelace. Jeannie and Jana have a heart for women and leading others to the freedom they have found in Jesus. They, too, know that life is hard, and the days can be long. A woman's heart, time, and attention can be pulled in so many directions. They know what it feels like, at times, to be merely surviving or simply managing from one task to the next. Jeannie and Jana assemble a lineup of women speakers who have earned the right to speak personally about sexual abuse, childhood and adult trauma, physical and emotional abuse, drug addiction, alcoholism, perfectionism, divorce, loss of children, grief, near-death medical diagnoses, depression, anxiety, post-traumatic stress disorder, affairs, abortion, and others.

Through their professions as clinical therapists, they have seen the depths of brokenness life can bring. But just as they have seen brokenness, they have seen triumph. Just as they have witnessed the heaviness of chains, they have witnessed the freedom that comes when those chains are broken. Just as they have witnessed loss and grief, they have witnessed healing and restoration. They have taken a front row seat in the lives of others, seeing how Jesus has healed, restored, and made new what the enemy meant for destruction—but they have also lived this journey in their own lives as Jesus delivered them from their own past and brokenness.

All too often, Christians have the idea that if their faith was stronger, they would not struggle. For example, the world often says, "If you have anxiety, your faith is not strong enough," or, "Christians should not be depressed." But what does the Bible say about mental health?

Jeannie and Jana have seen society attempt to disconnect spirituality and mental health. They value the local church, and it is their desire to come alongside and fight the battle of mental illness together, both with a spiritual lens as well as one that looks at the psychology of today's woman.

We limit ourselves as women, as busy moms or wives, as professionals, and as persons with depression or anxiety. But with God, there are NO LIMITS. This retreat is about *freedom*. Freedom to live without the chains of mental health difficulties like depression or anxiety. Freedom to live in your true Jesus-given identity. Freedom to live without the chains that have bound you, your mother, your sisters, or your daughters. Freedom to live in the way that Jesus meant for you to live. Jesus did not die for you to live this way. He died for you to live!

You can contact me for speaking events and retreats through A Servant's Heart with Jeannie Lynch at www. aservantsheartwithjeannielynch.com

Anything is Possible

"The Lord is close to the brokenhearted and saves those who are crushed in spirit."

Psalm 34:18

"The Spirit of the Sovereign Lord is on me, because the Lord has anointed me to proclaim good news to the poor. He sent me to bind up the brokenhearted, to proclaim freedom for the captives and release from darkness for the prisoners, to proclaim the year of the Lord's favor and the day of vengeance of our God, to comfort all who mourn, and provide for those who grieve in Zion—to bestow on them a crown of beauty instead of ashes, the oil of joy instead of mourning, and a garment of praise instead of a spirit of despair. They will be called oaks of righteousness, a planting of the Lord for the display of his splendor."

Isaiah 61:1-3

*E*ven when I felt utterly alone, I had a sense—just an inkling—that I was never truly alone.

I couldn't define it. It wasn't possible, being in so much pain. It was the way things were, the way things were always going to be. But through the first three decades of my life, and in the midst of complete desperation and desolation, it was there.

Rather, He was.

God was with me.

He was always there. I wasn't alone.

Not at all.

I look back now and see all the times where I should've caved in or even died. Abuse, numerous rejections, rape, a family suicide—every one of them happened and could've done me in. But they didn't. Somehow, some way, God took every hurtful event, every horror, and turned them around. He didn't create them. But He made each one of them stories and lessons that could be used for my good and to bring others to a place of freedom.

Evil became miracles.

I just had to not give up and not quit before the miracles manifested.

Back then and without my full knowledge, God had another purpose for me. He had a calling on my life. Sure, there were times I loathed myself. I hated who I had become. Yet there was also someone deep down within me who truly cared about people. Even loved them despite all of the hurt people had caused me. That conflict had waged within me ever since I could remember. It wasn't until I was 31, languishing in a jail cell after my third DUI, that I called out to God for help and for the first time felt, inexplicably, that I knew things were going to be okay. Propelled by that tiny act of faith and His response,

I was released from incarceration. From then on, I knew I was going to seek Him, and I pushed myself to get better.

I started developing a relationship with God. I learned He wasn't a punishing hellfire and brimstone tyrant but was loving and forgiving. As I began stripping my brain of all the things that had been in there prior, a healing started to take place within me that was profound. That deep desire to help people began to grow. I understood the saying, "But for the grace of God." Because of my gregarious personality and the things I'd been through, I started to believe I could really help people. I went back to school (years earlier, I had lied to my parents and told them I graduated when, actually, I had gone on a drunken binge during my last semester as an undergrad and never finished) because I realized I was supposed to be a counselor. I was not "saved." I hadn't yet accepted Jesus Christ as my Savior. But God *was* speaking to me. Guiding me. Loving me. Choosing me, even before I had chosen Him.

I got my bachelor's degree in psychology all while staying sober. I excelled in school. I didn't know I was smart until that time. Then, the North Carolina Vocational Rehab program paid for me to finish my undergraduate studies and remain in school two more years to get my master's degree at the University of West Georgia in Carrollton, Georgia. It was the first time in the program's history that they paid for someone to go out of state for a master's degree. Even before I graduated, I was already working at a dual diagnosis center where I was functionally the clinical director.

It was insane. Unheard of. A God thing. One of the many miracles to come. I was becoming the person that God had called me to become.

But I'm getting ahead of myself—and the story. All of

that, and so much more before and since, will be unfolded to you in the pages to come.

The miracles of God.

* * *

Today, I'm a Jesus-loving, belly-laughing, friend-hanging, single woman who loves people and animals. I fight for and love God's children who feel so broken that giving up appears to be their only option. I do this as a licensed professional counselor anointed to be a conduit of God as the Holy Spirit works through me to help people heal. The majority of my clients are dealing with dual diagnosis (addiction with mental illness) encompassing co-dependency, adult and childhood sexual trauma, and issues related to abuse—and why wouldn't they be. After all, I'd been through what they had, and I suffered from my own dual diagnosis of major depressive disorder, post-traumatic stress disorder, and a severe addiction to alcohol and drugs. Another avenue where God has taken the brokenness of my own personal experiences to help others is the No Limits Women's Conferences, LLC, an organization that exists to bridge the gap between life's struggles for women and spirituality, that I co-founded with Dr. Jana Lovelace.

While I know God has healed me, I still deal with the aftereffects from the traumas which shifted my brain chemistry, as I am on an anti-depressant and continue to remain aware of the condition of my mental health. I talk about these things openly and honestly because God told me many years ago that I was going to be used to educate people to reduce the stigma that still exist about mental illness and the treatment of such. As is the case with so many other people, my traumas began early and came often. They shaped my childhood and the early years of my adult life in tragic ways, as you will learn. But they did not define me. Instead, they serve to inform me as I help people through my therapy practice, Jeannie Lynch, LPC-S, NCC, LLC. He sends me the exact people I need to see. I've always had what feels like instinct when treating clients, but I know it's the Holy Spirit. He tells me stuff during a session. We have it down to an art where there's not even a pause. I'd like to take credit for this because it is so cool, but it is not me. It is Him, and it is awesome.

I'm stepping out of my comfort zone like never before, also overseeing a women's small group through my church called the Sprouts. Through it all, I'm realizing that I am a natural born leader. I didn't know that because my voice had been stolen from me, but over time and through His healing, God has given me back my voice, restored it to health, and called me to be a leader of women. I am convinced that the Lord is calling a lot of women to exemplify principles of character, authenticity, and servant-heartedness, but feelings stop them. We are to follow the truth of God's Word, not our feelings. That is "God-fidence," where we do not have confidence in ourselves or our own ability, but in Him.

And that's the thing I've learned. It's all about Him. If God can heal me, He can heal any one of us. God loves broken people. He is all about coming into our lives and healing us from the inside out. In turn, He will use the testimony of our stories to further His Kingdom.

Just don't quit before the miracle happens. That's what I've been telling my clients now for over 30 years because it's true! As I wrote in the book, *Women in Leadership—Living*

Beyond Challenges, "God was the catalyst to my healing. If human beings could do to me what was done to me, I wanted no part of the human race. I was a tough cookie, and I wasn't going to let anyone get close to me. I had to learn God's grace and mercy. It has been tough, but it had to be tough in order for me to comprehend. For myself or anyone who has been through similar traumas and challenges, I can say without any hesitation that anything is possible with God. Don't give up. You can heal and live in freedom. You do not have to remain a victim of your past." I'll add here that your future doesn't have to look like your past 30 years.

All of the events of my life are the pieces of who I really am as a person, and I firmly believe God has used them for my good and the good of others (Romans 8:28). I am able to share my past struggles with others who may be having similar experiences, and the beauty of it is that I can honestly say, "If I can do it, so can you."

You can trust Him. He is trustworthy. I can also say, from a place of rawness in my heart, that I have forgiven every single individual who brought me harm. I cannot express to you what that means: true freedom.

But I'm going to try—and as I do, I hope the story of my life inspires you and convinces you that you, too, are not alone.

Not at all.

Chapter 1

Foreboding Beginnings

"For you created my inmost being; you knit me together in my mother's womb. I praise you because I am fearfully and wonderfully made; your works are wonderful, I know that full well. My frame was not hidden from you when I was made in the secret place, when I was woven together in the depths of the earth. Your eyes saw my unformed body; all the days ordained for me were written in your book before one of them came to be."

Psalm 139:13-16

I am of the firm belief, because I see it almost every day in my practice, that our earliest childhood memories shape our foundational belief systems, for good or for bad. That we are alone. That we are not good enough. That we are not lovable. We carry those key remembrances into our adulthood, and they become who we are.

I know I did.

My first memory was particularly telling. I was two-and-a-half years old, and I was at my oldest sister Lois Jean's home in Greenbelt, Maryland where I would go for babysitting when my mother went to work. It was very cold that day, and I was outside waving goodbye to my mother as she started to drive off. As I backed away from my mother's vehicle, I suddenly slipped and fell backwards into a tree well, a cinder block pit around the base of the trunk. It was only a couple of feet deep, but as far as I was concerned it might as well have been a cavernous sinkhole that suddenly opened up beneath me. I remember bawling and feeling utterly abandoned as I desperately watched my mother's car pull away, even as Lois's husband bent down and pulled me out of the well. I hit my head on the tree and was pretty banged up, but I was already crying because my mom was leaving me, and I didn't like being at Lois Jean's house.

I wasn't treated well there.

Lois Jean, her husband, and their three boys would move in with us a few months later because she was ailing with a rare and serious curvature of the spine. Some paralysis from the condition had already begun by then, and she'd already had one surgery where the doctors believed she wouldn't survive the procedure. But Lois Jean was tough, and she'd need to be. She'd have several more surgeries in the years to come during which two of her ribs and one lung had to be removed because of the curvature. Before it was all over, the entire right side of her body would end up paralyzed.

My second memory, when I was three, took place at our house shortly after Lois Jean had moved in. I was getting my mouth washed out with soap along with Lois Jean's boys. I recall sensing that it wasn't fair, that somehow, I didn't do what I was accused of doing.

I wasn't heard, and I certainly wasn't believed.

The third memory came when I was given my first Holy Communion in the Catholic church. I was one of those kids who liked to understand what I was doing, so I asked the nun to explain to me what happened in the confessional box. The nun, who I later concluded likely had a mental health condition, must've been in one of her more negative moments. "If you don't understand," she announced sternly, her long, black cape swooping toward me with the force of her declaration, "then you are going to hell!" I saw her as a right-hand representative of God, so her words went straight through to my core, even if I wouldn't fully understand why until much later. I thought she could peer into my very soul and see that I was bad—and, therefore, God saw me as being bad.

The idea that terrible things happened to me because I was bad stuck with me for years.

They may not sound like much, but let me tell you, each one was significant. As a result of that trio of memories, and others that accompanied them, I felt alone and unable to get close to anyone for years—not until God healed me from those ingrained feelings.

* * *

I was a late baby. My mother, Dorothy, was 42 and my father, Willie, was 50 when I was born in Washington, D.C. My sisters, Mary Virginia and Lois Jean, were 16 and 22 respectively at the time, and they fought over what I was going to be named. Complete opposites, they both wanted me to be named after them, so my parents came up with a compromise incorporating each of their names into my name: Jean Marie. The first place we lived was in Takoma Park, which is considered to be in Maryland but is part of the D.C. metropolitan area. I don't remember it much, but my mom told me I used to call it "the dark house." I think it was because it had shutters on the windows that kept the light out. We moved to Bethesda and into a large, split-level house to better accommodate Lois Jean and her family. They lived downstairs while we took the second floor, but we shared meals together. All of us there in one house, it was something.

I truly adored my parents. They were very good people, and they were devout in their faith. I loved and honored them. My mom was raised in West Virginia and was the middle of eight children. All of five-foot-three, she was definitely not skinny, but she wasn't heavy, either. Strong and sturdy with a gentle face, she had blue eyes and was a curly carrot top whose hair turned a brilliant white as she aged. For the longest time, mom wore traditional dresses until switching to a more contemporary blouse and slacks look by the time I was a teen. She was quite attractive. Mom was also a master bridge player who taught others how to play, and she played basketball and softball as a kid. As an adult, she coached both sports in a huge church league outside the D.C. area.

Sadly, mom suffered greatly with postpartum depression after I was born. In fact, Mary Virginia was my primary caretaker for a while because mom's depression was so severe. When I was two, Mary Virginia got married and moved about 30 minutes away, and my relationship with her was distant for a long time after that. I was introduced to depression as a small child because of my mother's issues, but I quickly learned not to cry. Crying was seen as a sign of weakness. If I cried, my family shamed me into stopping, probably because each one of them had problems showing their emotions. Lois Jean's boys, who were nine weeks, two-and-a-half years, and three-and-a-half years older than me, also picked on me if I showed any sign of weakness. So, I stopped crying at age three and didn't shed another tear for 30 years, so pent up were my emotions.

When Lois Jean and her family came to live with us, mom became the primary caregiver for everyone, and it was a full house to say the least. Mom cooked, washed, helped my sister, and made sure the boys were taken care of. I know I played with my nephews, but I didn't feel I fit in. In fact, it was more like I was adopted. I was always with my mother, and she was a real go-getter, but one of the things I remember most poignantly about my childhood was a sense of being alone and wondering where everybody was. Mom was simply so busy keeping a household and taking care of my sister and her boys while her husband worked, I didn't get enough of her attention. She worked at the National Education Association in D.C., one of several ladies that ran the organization, and while I don't recall her title, I do remember that she once interviewed with then Senator Richard Nixon to become his personal secretary. My mother was very smart. She could type and transcribe and had wonderful work skills despite all her labors at home. She was offered the job but declined due to just having given birth to me.

Later, when I was a young adult, my mom often told me, "Thank goodness you were a good baby," and she'd describe herself sitting down holding and occupying my sister's three boys while patting me with her foot as I laid on the floor. She was a very good-hearted woman, probably to a fault. Some of my fondest memories were with her. I have a picture of me and my mom cutting grass when I was maybe four years old. Well, actually, I was pushing a baby carriage, but I thought I was cutting the grass. Mom had a push mower. To this day, I still love cutting grass, although it's on a riding mower now. I cut six acres every week. Oddly, it's therapy for me, and it's where some of my most profound revelations from God have come.

My dad was born in Washington D.C., the second youngest of ten children. He, too, was a spitfire and served as a deputy superintendent of operations in the D.C. school system. He went into the city every weekday eight-to-five to go to work, then spent his Saturdays away from home playing golf. At five-foot-eight, dad was five inches taller than mom, but he was lean and athletic. Both mom and dad coached fifth-to-sixth grade girls in the softball and basketball church league when he wasn't on the golf course. When he went to work and church, dad wore a suit and bow tie that provided a dapper foundation for his handsome, kind face, blue eyes, and curly, dark red hair.

Dad wasn't around a whole lot, but from a very early age, not much older than three or four, I remember being with him out in the back yard or at the nearby playground hitting golf balls. He cut down a set of wooden clubs for me, and I had my own golf bag. We'd hit regulation balls back and forth to each other, catching them with a baseball glove. I had a natural gift for the game, and dad just loved that. Whenever we went to the playground, he let me sit on his lap as we drove back home. I'd put my hands on the wheel like I was driving the car, and I thought that was better than sliced bread. That was our time together, and I treasured it. But between his work and time away at the golf course, and mom taking care of everything else and working, too, I was mostly on my own.

Because my mother and father were such giving people, they couldn't imagine not taking in my sister to help take care of her and her family. I appreciated their heart, and I don't want to seem ungrateful. But taking in Lois Jean's family kind of ripped my childhood from me. Otherwise, I would've had more of my parents—and may have avoided the horrors I experienced as a child.

*　*　*

From age four until about age ten, I was sexually abused by family members both male and female. To this day, I don't have absolute, concrete memories of the abuse, but I know that it happened. If God ever wants me to experience the full memories, He'll allow it. Otherwise, I'm not seeking to draw them out. I know what I do to the extent that I do, and I have used that pain to foster healing in others.

But that healing wouldn't come for me until much later. In the meantime, the abuse tainted me and informed my life, defining who I was, just as much, if not more, than my other early childhood memories did. I internalized the feelings that something was wrong with me and that I was not lovable. I concluded that I was alone because I was unlovable.

That foundational belief system was already underway at age five when I started school. I entered first grade in a public school a block away from my home in Bethesda. I began acting out when I was eight with my teachers by rebelling, disrespecting them, and basically being a little brat. I remember criticizing a belief of someone who was Jewish. I didn't believe in God or Jesus or whatever. If someone said, "This is important to me." I'd respond, "Well, that's a bunch of crap." It was not really *like* me to do that, but the acting out was indicative of what was happening *to* me at home. I was easily irritated and knew that I didn't feel good about myself.

In fifth grade, I was enrolled in the small Catholic school that my nephews were already attending, and I promptly upped my bad behavior and fell in with some unruly peers. I was a holy terror, especially with the nuns. I struggled as a student, too. I didn't read well, and I probably would have been diagnosed with ADHD (inattentive type) had it been years later. However, I believe my classroom struggles were an extension of the depression I was experiencing. That underachievement, though, was offset by how gifted I was as an athlete. I started formally playing sports in fourth grade, and as I continued, I was head and shoulders above the rest, and why not? I was a coach's kid, so I already had all the fundamentals down because I had been to every gym and softball field there was. I was taken to all of the practices and games. That was supposed to be our "family time," but while I was with my parents, they were always coaching, so I certainly didn't perceive it that way.

There was one time in particular when I recall being at the high school softball field. It was cold—bitterly cold, the chill wind cutting like knife edges across my face. I was hungry and off to the side sitting by myself, and though there were kids all around being coached by my mom and dad, I felt utterly alone. The sadness was so overwhelming, the sound of the big white balls striking the leather of the gloves was strangely muted, like distant punches trying to break through the suffocating blanket of despair that engulfed me.

I would've liked somebody to come over to see me or offer to play with me. However, I was younger than the girls they were coaching, and they didn't want to have anything to do with me. But what I wanted even more than being noticed by the other girls was the attention and love of my parents. Looking back, I recognize that I wanted them to *choose* me. I wanted them to say, "We need to make Jeannie our priority rather than the children we are coaching and our grandchildren." I was surrounded by people, but I was achingly lonely. It was a theme that continued throughout my life, of being alone and feeling unlovable.

I had one best friend, Colleen, from fourth through seventh grade. We played basketball and softball together, my parents were our coaches, and we played on the same teams. She was a year ahead of me in school and two years older than me. We were thick as thieves. She helped me feel a bit less lonely.

I remember having conversations with Colleen as a kid, many of them revealing how I thought I had feelings for her. She tried to explain to me that her feelings were not like mine—that how she felt about boys was different than how she felt about me. I couldn't understand. Neither one of us understood, really. It was hard, and while Colleen was truly a gem, never making me feel judged or unwanted because of my feelings, there was still a lot of shame in that for me.

That was my first instance of same sex attraction, and it wouldn't be my last. Did I know where it came from, if it was a predisposition, or if the abuse played a part? I had no idea then, and I didn't for years because my point of reference always had sexual abuse in it. Nor did I know then if I was trying to get some emotional need met. I just know that I really thought I was attracted to her.

From late elementary school onward, I excelled in sports. In ninth grade, I played basketball and ran track. The next year I played tennis, golf, basketball, and softball, and lettered in every sport. I later played volleyball in college. My sophomore year in high school, my coach told me I was supposed to receive an award for being the top female athlete in the school, but I didn't get it because my behavior was so bad. That was a big letdown because I knew I was by far the best all-around athlete. My skill in sports caused a lot of jealousy among my classmates. They wanted to say it was because I was a coach's kid and I was shown favoritism. The truth was it was harder for me because I was the coach's kid. My family made sure they weren't going to show me anything even close to favoritism. I had to constantly prove myself to them, particularly with my sister.

Before her spinal condition, Lois Jean was also a good athlete. Through her tenacity, she carried on as a basketball and softball coach, and she ended up coaching me, even with her paralysis. She never gave me a break. She coached the seventh-to-eighth grade girls basketball team, and she wanted to move me up from the fifth-to-sixth grade squad, even though I would've been really good if I'd been kept where I was. But then Lois Jean never put me into the game. Everybody knew I was the best player on the team, yet there I sat on the bench. I wasn't angry about it, but it made no sense at all. Even the other players couldn't understand why she kept me on the bench.

Finally, we were in the city championship game, and we were losing. Near the end of the game, Lois Jean finally put me in. We were down by ten points, and I scored eight, but we still lost by two. I imagine she was desperate and hoped I'd help us win, or maybe she knew I *wouldn't* be able to pull the win out and just wanted me to suffer. Later, mom told me Lois Jean kept me on the bench that season because she didn't want to show me any favoritism. I just think she was jealous of me and may have wanted me to fail. I'll never know for sure.

So, despite my talent, even how I looked at myself as an athlete began to negatively affect me. I came to believe that my sense of how my parents valued me rested on my athletic ability—so I made athleticism my identity for years to follow. Everybody in my family played sports, even Lois Jean's three boys. Being the youngest, sports were how I received approval and validation. My parents didn't bolster me up, though. My dad never told me how good I was. One of the reasons I later quit golf as a freshman in college was because it was no longer fun with my father's persistent lack of affirmation and overt criticism.

I went to the Catholic school until eighth grade before returning to public school for my high school years in Sanford, North Carolina. We moved there about three years after my father's retirement because, as a golfer, he wanted to live further south. We had tried to get me into a Catholic high school in D.C. noted for the success of its athletic programs, but it wouldn't take me because of my behavioral issues. When that failed, my parents felt the timing was right for the move. By then, Lois Jean and her family had relocated into their own home in Bethesda, and they remained in Maryland when we left. With her boys being older, my parents felt it was time for them to be on their own and for us to do our thing. Lois Jean was stable at the time of our move, though the right side of her body was pretty much fully paralyzed. I didn't really want much to do with her. We didn't talk on the phone at all, but she talked to my mother almost every day. I wouldn't see Lois Jean again for many years, and when I did, it would be for a horrible reason.

Meanwhile, I actually started seeing Mary Virginia again because her youngest son, Rob, came to spend the summers with my parents, and my sister and her family visited for the holidays. She'd had a history of depression ever since she was a child, and I knew mom and dad had often checked in with Mary Virginia over the years after she moved away from us because she and her husband had a rocky relationship. They fought like hell. Still, even though Mary Virginia was there occasionally, I maintained my distance from my sisters. I wanted to. I'd always loved Mary Virginia, but I did not miss Lois Jean.

*   *   *

Being in North Carolina was certainly a shock to the system. I went from a small Catholic school of 250 and living in the suburbs of D.C. to a big high school in small-town USA with a freshman class of 500. It had a good athletics program, would finish state runners-up in golf, and three years later win the state title during my time on the team, and it was just starting a women's basketball squad. But the culture there was so unlike what I was used to. I felt like I had taken a step back 25 years in time. People said, "Hey," and waved at you going down the road. I'd go, "Hey, what?" We didn't wave at random people where I came from. It was Southern hospitality, but it was weird. At school, I often had to deal with two very mean girls who each had the same gang of followers.

Because I was the new kid on the block, they thought I was an easy target, and they tried to bully me.

Notice I said "tried." Since I was an athlete, their strategy was to get me by myself so it could be several against one. I never threw the first blow, but I did not wait for the second one. I simply picked out the main leader and went after her. I was not a fighter, but I was when I had to be, and whenever I did, it didn't go too well for them. In ninth grade, when I was the only freshman to be a starter on the varsity basketball team, I was hanging out with some older kids shooting hoops. One of those girls was there, and she had a major chip on her shoulder that day. As I went up for a shot, she sucker punched me right in the stomach. That was a mistake. When she did that, it was all over. I jumped on her. She got in one punch, and I got in many. She left me alone after that.

In short order, the move to North Carolina became disheartening. It was as though I was all by myself again. There was a void. Something was wrong with me, and I was not okay. I know now that I felt *less* than unlovable. Of course, by then I was drinking—and it's a testament to my physical ability (or a miracle) that I achieved anything as an athlete considering how much alcohol I was consuming.

I had my first drink all the way back when I was ten. It was from a champagne fountain at a New Year's Eve party my parents hosted—and from then on, I was hooked. I could drink an exorbitant amount of booze. By age 13, when we arrived in North Carolina, I was drinking beer every weekend. By 14, I had totaled my boyfriend's car. That was crazy. I'd just started tenth grade, and this boyfriend (I'd already had a couple other boyfriends before him, always older than me) let me drive his car, a deep burgundy Ford Maverick with a black vinyl top, with two of my closest friends, Nan and Tammy. The three of us were all in the same class, and we had a lot of the same friends. We were drinking cheap wine and smoking cigars. Suddenly, my stogie dropped to the floor from my right hand, and I bent down to pick it up, forgetting I was behind the wheel. We tore through one side of a split rail fence, darted into a pasture, and then plunged through the fence on the other side. Despite the fact that it was a single car accident, it's a miracle none of us were hurt.

The police came. It was my first experience with the law. When my boyfriend arrived at the scene, he wasn't exactly gallant. He was about to turn 18, and he denied he even knew me. I had some choice words for him later, though maybe I should've been kinder. After all, I didn't even have a driver's license, and he still let me borrow his car. Mom made me go to school the next Monday. I begged her not to because it was a large school with almost 3,000 kids, and everybody was talking about it. Even the teachers knew, and I didn't like that kind of attention. I don't remember what the legal outcome was from that night, but I did have to go to court. My friends, Nan and Tammy, weren't allowed by their parents to hang out with me anymore after that, either. That hurt like hell—and there I was again, surrounded by people yet all alone, as a result of my own bratty behaviors and doing things to consistently push others away. But, of course, I didn't own that at the time.

I was having blackouts by then, too. I'll never forget the aftermath of one instance when I was a little older. I had a bad habit of skipping school on Fridays. Lots of students did. Whoever wanted to skip went down to the senior parking lot, and we'd drive off to all sorts of different places, like a regular "field trip." We'd be drinking, of course, and this one time we were playing the "turtle game." It's a drinking game where you have to repeat a series of phrases such as "one red hen, two brown bear, three running hare" that become more complex, like, "six simple Simons sitting on a stoop." The more inebriated you are, the harder it is to say them. The person who knows all of the phrases is the head turtle. Every time you begin a phrase, you must take a drink. If you mess up the phrase, you must take a drink. If you want help from the head turtle, you must take a drink.

It was easy to see how this was going to go, and I was drinking guys under the table. But at some point, I went into a blackout, and while I was out, school officials came and caught us. I don't remember seeing them, talking to them, or anything else about it. All I knew was when I got home, I had one shoe on and one shoe off because when I woke up the next morning, I couldn't find one of my best tennis shoes. I knew something wasn't good. Confused, I snuck out to the carport to make sure my car was in the driveway because I didn't remember driving home. Being a blackout drinker is a yucky feeling. When it happens, you have absolutely no recollection of what you did. That's devastating because people think you are aware of what you're doing and that you're being yourself when you really aren't. Years later, in my sobriety, some of my blackouts came back to me. I wish they had stayed away. I was never doing anything good.

The next night, one of my friends called to ask what I was going to tell the assistant principal, Mr. Alexander.

"What are you talking about?" I asked. I didn't even know my mother and I had an appointment with the assistant principal.

"Jeannie, you got caught!"

I knew I was going to be in a crapload of trouble. My mother and I went in Monday morning, and we took our seats across from Mr. Alexander's desk. I hadn't prepared her for what was going to happen. How could I, since I couldn't remember it anyway.

"I understand you and Mike were playing a drinking game called the turtle game," he began.

I knew he was telling the truth. He had no reason to lie, and Mike was a very good friend of mine. It was horrible.

I sat there silently, knowing my mother would be upset and embarrassed, and she was.

I was supposed to have been suspended from school for three days, but the suspension was later shortened because it was going to interfere with a softball game, and they wanted me to be able to play.

It was funny in a way. There I was, the all-American athlete, but I was pushing the limits and taking risks. I had this Dr. Jekyll and Mr. Hyde personality when I drank. I couldn't tell you what I was going to do or where I would end up once I got started. I was up for any dare, such as riding on the back of a speeding car. I got several concussions from doing things like that.

* * *

Becoming alcoholic made sense in that it ran in my family—though I didn't find out about that until after that accident with my boyfriend's car. That's when my mother told me that my father had a drinking problem. She called him a binge drinker and revealed that she had actually asked him to leave until he went to the Catholic church and took a pledge of sobriety with a priest. He came home saying he had taken a one-year pledge, and she told him that wasn't good enough. It had to be for life. He went back to the priest, did that, and she said he never took another drink again. He had all the -isms of a typical alcoholic—he was overly critical, a perfectionist, and he had silent anger—but he didn't drink.

I was surprised by the revelation in that I had never actually seen my father drink. Yet when I found out, I didn't see that he had a drinking problem. I didn't think he was an alcoholic any more than I thought I was. It's heartbreaking. I was involved with coaches, teachers, church, all kinds of things. Everybody knew the trouble I was getting into, but nobody said anything. I was a severe alcoholic in high school. Somebody should have said something. But they didn't. That's one reason I am so hard-nosed with adolescents today. I push them hard about substance abuse because I needed someone to push me and nobody did. Even mom, seeing what dad did and what I was doing, didn't do anything to address the problems. It was just too much for her. She didn't want to face it.

In retrospect, I was just like my father. I was a binge drinker. It was like I had a hollow leg. But I hid it well from my family, or thought I did. I could drink large amounts and still look okay, but the fact was, I was spiraling out of control.

Today, I understand that the alcoholism in my family was a generational curse, the kind that progresses from parent to child without skipping a beat. We came across as the clean-cut, all-American family, but it was being kept in the dark—reminiscent of the literal darkness that shrouded my very first home when I was tiny. That's where Satan, the enemy, operates. Addiction ran all through my father's side of the family. Two of his brothers were killed in car accidents, probably under the influence. There was mental illness, too. I was older by the time I learned all of this, and it was very well hidden. It was something people didn't talk about, kept silent primarily because of shame. You don't air your dirty laundry. The only other person I remember being intoxicated in my family was Lois' husband. He was a happy drunk but, boy, could he put it away. He lost jobs over his drinking, including one in a school because he was letting the younger kids drink with him. Lois tried to hide all of that, of course, but I can look back now and see what was going on clear as day.

Leading up to graduating from high school in 1976 and going to junior college, I was drinking pretty much all the time in the evenings, partying, and raising H-E-double toothpicks. No matter what was going on, I wouldn't drink the night before a game. But I'd certainly drink the night after playing. Around that same time, Mary Virginia had a double mastectomy and shortly thereafter a quadruple bypass. Mary was 32 years old. She came and recouped with my mom and dad after I had left for college. She and her husband divorced, and within a short period of time, Mary remarried a man a few years older than me, but significantly younger than herself.

I stayed in North Carolina and went to Louisburg College on a basketball scholarship. The coach asked me to sign up for volleyball, too, and within six weeks I had a starting position on the squad, even though I had never played volleyball before. Louisburg was a private Methodist school, but that doesn't mean we behaved like wholesome, young Methodists should. Quite the con- trary. We snuck boys into our rooms all the time to drink and party. We spread hot water mixed with dishwashing liquid on the hallway floors, stripped down to our bras and panties, and then slid up and down the corridors. We had fun, and it really kept the floors clean, too.

I was quite the practical joker, especially with firecrackers. I learned that if I placed a still-warm cigarette filter against the fuse, it delayed the lighting and detonation of the firecracker until I was well clear of the scene of the crime. Sometimes, I'd set up a butt and firecracker on the end of a string, go to a window, and then drop it on a line down to the floor below and tap it on the window. *Boom!* I especially loved when the girls were downstairs in the lobby playing spades. I'd go down, light one up in the nearby restroom, and already be back up in my room when I'd hear it go off. Everyone screamed and ran out of the building. It was absolutely hilarious to me in the midst of my rebellion.

Other than my shenanigans, my freshman year was without major incident except for one night when me and two other basketball players came back from a night in Raleigh, North Carolina. We were crazy drunk and in the rear of an old dormitory that had a brick-enclosed fire escape. I was three stories up, standing up on top of the platform, raising hell and making all kinds of noise, so much so that most of my teammates and others in the dorm were trying to get me to quiet down. Before I knew it, I fell backward and plunged downward six feet—how I didn't fall all the way to the first floor, I don't know—and I hit my head super hard on the metal platform until my face was starting to turn blue when the co-captain of the team gave me mouth-to-mouth resuscitation. My coach was so mad, he wanted to kick me off the team. Both captains, including the one who saved me, insisted he give me another chance.

As punishment, I had to sit out one game with the two others who went out with me that night. I pretended I was injured so I didn't have to answer questions about why I wasn't playing. I couldn't allow myself to be vulnerable enough to fess up to my behavior.

Everybody on campus came to know me either from sports, partying, or being a joker, and most everyone liked me because I was playful and really cared about people. Too bad I didn't bother to extend that same level of care to myself and my responsibilities as my sophomore year got underway. Because I partied so much, missed so many classes, and did so poorly in school my first year, I wasn't allowed to play basketball for the first part of my sophomore year. That nearly killed me, and I decided to do everything I could to bring up my grades. In the meantime, we had new family drama at Christmas. I have a poignant picture of Mary Virginia sitting on the couch in my parent's living room, having slashed through the tendons on both arms in an attempt to commit suicide. She was wearing a medical apparatus designed to help her arms heal.

That was hard. No one in my family would talk about it. It was the pink elephant in the room. It always had been. She had tried to commit suicide a number of other times when I was a kid, though no one ever told me about it then. I remember thinking, "This is jacked up." By then, my relationship with Mary Virginia was distant and her health was worse. She was just 36. Looking back today, I believe it was all from depression. Mary Virginia was never happy.

As my second semester got underway, my grades had improved and I started playing basketball again, all while keeping up my insane behavior. One night, I led five of us girls, drunk as could be, on a quest. We dressed in black, borrowed one of the girls' cars, a hatchback, and went to the fenced area behind a grocery store where they stored all the empty deposit bottles. They were worth a lot of money, so we set up a human conveyor line, with me closest to the store. In no time, we loaded up the hatchback with at least $750 in soda bottles. We stashed them in a nearby pasture and decided to head back for more. When we returned, the owner charged out of the two metal doors at the rear of the store, shotgun in hand. "Hold it, you sons of bitches!" he yelled, and then fired. He probably thought we were guys.

To say the least, we went straight to jail that night, my first stay behind bars, but I told the girls not to worry: we'd simply use the money from the looted bottles for court fees.

No, we wouldn't. When we went out to gather up our bottled bounty the next evening, they were gone. Someone had showed up and stolen our stolen bottles! How dare they steal from us! Oh, the irony and the criminal mind. We never found out who robbed us.

* * *

I totally let school go and partied my butt off day and night after basketball season ended. I didn't crack a book from that time on. I don't think I passed a single class. For its part, the basketball team finished first in the conference and second in the region. We were nationally recognized, a top team, and I was a baller on a team filled with them. But that was the last sport I ever played as a college athlete. Louisburg was only a two-year school, I had to transfer to keep competing, but no one wanted me. Not even my athletic prowess was good enough to attract another school to recruit me. My bad behavior and poor academics had finally caught up to me.

When junior college ended at age 19, I responded by getting lost in a whirlwind of drugs and alcohol because I thought my athletic career was over. Who was I if not an athlete? How would my parents love and accept me if not through athletics? How would anyone else accept me? I was lost without my sports.

I had not used drugs until this time. Subconsciously, I somehow already anticipated the severity of the drug addict that I would quickly become. Devastated, I also went into a serious identity crisis that was going to deepen my depression, sustain my heavy drinking, dangerously accelerate my drug use, and countdown to one of the single worst moments of my life.

Chapter 2

Delving into Devastation

"As for you, you were dead in your transgressions and sins, in which you used to live when you followed the ways of this world and of the ruler of the kingdom of the air, the spirit who is now at work in those who are disobedient. All of us also lived among them at one time, gratifying the cravings of our flesh and following its desires and thoughts. Like the rest, we were by nature deserving of wrath. But because of his great love for us, God, who is rich in mercy, made us alive with Christ even when we were dead in transgressions—it is by grace you have been saved. And God raised us up with Christ and seated us with him in the heavenly realms in Christ Jesus, in order that in the coming ages he might show the incomparable riches of his grace, expressed in his kindness to us in Christ Jesus. For it is by

*grace you have been saved, through faith—and this is not
from yourselves, it is the gift of God—not by works, so that
no one can boast."*

Ephesians 2:1-9

I started mixing drugs with alcohol, and within two
months' time I was sticking a needle in my arm. I
shot up methylenedioxyamphetamine, or MDA,
a psychedelic closely related to Ecstasy, with a heroin base.
I used cocaine and crank, which is a methamphetamine
base, and mescaline. I was chasing the high because I
didn't want to deal with the end of my athletic career or
my lack of identity. All I wanted was to feel better, and in
doing so, push away my depression. I avoided my emotional pain at all costs.

I didn't realize I would soon pay a much greater cost.

In no time, I became a full-blown addict. I was living in
a three-bedroom apartment on Wrightsville Beach, North
Carolina with two other girls I first met at Louisburg.
There were probably about 40 of us that lived along the
beach, and we were all dopers. I worked waiting tables,
though I wasn't at all consistent with that. I was far better
with hanging out at a bar called The Crest. My friends
and I loved going there to keep the party going. One
night in June, I had taken 10 pills of valium, each one 10
milligrams, at the same time I was drinking alcohol. To
put that in perspective, a regular dose of valium is one 10
milligram pill every four to six hours. I had ten times the
amount of valium in my system than normal.

I should not have been breathing, much less walking,
but that's how high my drug tolerance had become—and
how reckless I was getting. I mean, with that amount of
poison in my system, I should've been dead. But when

you're an abuse victim, like I was stemming back to my childhood, you do things that are high-risk, not so much because you're consciously suicidal, but subconsciously, you *are* trying to kill yourself, if for no other reason than to numb the pain.

I wouldn't have told anyone I wanted to die. But I surely did not care if I lived.

My choice to do the drug/alcohol combo got me barred from The Crest. Anybody who looked at me knew I was in a drug stupor. One of my closest friends was a bartender there and probably gave them a heads up on how bad I was. Since she had given me a ride to the bar that evening, when I was told to leave, she gave me the keys to her car. As I pulled out onto the main road, I hit a police car. I was so high I didn't even know where I was at that point.

The officer administered a breathalyzer test, and because it only measures alcohol, I didn't blow enough to be considered intoxicated. But it was clear I was under the influence and then some from the addition of the valium. Since it's illegal in North Carolina for anyone younger than 21 to drive with any detectable amount of an illicit or otherwise prohibited drug, I was charged with my first DUI. I went to jail again, they impounded my friend's car, and some other friends had to come with the bond money to get me released before I went to court. As I was leaving, one of the officers commented to one of my friends, "She'll be back!"

He was right. He knew I was on a course of self-destruction. I probably did, too. I simply didn't want to acknowledge it.

I lost my driver's license, but I continued to drive illegally anyway. While I was occasionally staying in touch with them, I didn't tell my parents about any of this. I didn't want anyone or anything to get in the way of what I was doing. Substances had become my only way of coping, and I did not want any lectures. I couldn't handle hearing how desperate and distressed my parents were with me.

In stark contrast to the rest of my behavior, my virginity was very important to me. I had determined that I was going to remain a virgin until I got married. After that first expression of same sex attraction as a kid to Colleen, I found myself attracted to both boys and girls, but my only significant relationship was with a boy, dating back a couple of years to right after high school. He was about six years older than me, and I really liked him. We'd end up having an on-again, off-again relationship that would have serious repercussions later, but during this period of my life, we did not have sex.

Maybe it was my strict religious upbringing that made me want to remain celibate. Perhaps it was that both of my sisters got pregnant before they married, and our parents did not condone premarital sex. Or, it may simply have been that I feared the vulnerability of an actual relationship that I was convinced could only end in rejection.

Whatever the case, even as I was mired in addiction and struggling with my self-identity, that desire to remain a virgin persisted—until it was cruelly and violently taken from me.

*   *   *

In February 1979, at 20 years of age, during a snowstorm in a trailer outside of Raleigh, I was raped and beaten by multiple perpetrators to the point that I was unrecognizable and left for dead. I still don't recall why I was at the trailer or who precisely was there. I do remember when I came to, sat up, and realized that I was completely naked and my body hurt, that the first thing I saw was blood on the walls. *My* blood.

Shame surged through me and over me, emptying me of everything except an overwhelming sense of guilt. *This happened because of who I am*, I thought. *This is my fault. God, why didn't you allow them to just kill me?*

While I didn't find out the extent of my injuries from the rape until much later, I surely would have died from what I suffered. But my true brokenness shattered me far deeper than my physical wounds. I was totally void, like a cold, dry wind had just blown through my very soul. *If human beings can do this to one another, I want no part of it.* At that moment, my humanity was stripped away. Everything worth anything was gone. There was nothing left inside of me.

After the attack, I stayed holed up in my apartment for the next six months and tried desperately to bury what had happened, doing only what I had to do to make ends meet until I recovered from my injuries. My roommates were upset and wanted to beat some butt to take revenge. I had to beg and plead with them to just leave it alone. After that, they never talked about the assault around me because I wouldn't allow them to do so. They were also worried about me becoming pregnant or contracting a sexually transmitted disease, but I couldn't care less. I never told anyone in my family about what happened. I was so stunted by the trauma that I didn't really have a response to it. I was too busy avoiding it.

I did have one reaction, though. As others brought drugs or booze into the apartment, we used—I mean *used*. It wasn't fun any longer. It wasn't meant to be. I just wanted not to feel. I even did a speed ball, a combination of cocaine and heroin, in both arms at the same time. It felt like my heart was going to burst out of my chest. I could've, should've, overdosed at any time. I had hit an all-new low. I was going into oblivion.

All my life I had felt unloved by others. Now, for the first time, I felt the same way about myself and that I deserved to feel that way. This was different, a deeper low in my sea of lows.

I was a shell of a human being. The essence of Jeannie was gone.

From then on, I had no regard for myself or my safety. I used to hang out at a biker bar called The Alibi. Out back was the area where they parked all their "fat boys," the massive Harleys and other motorcycles they drove, thousands of dollars of rumbling machines. Meanwhile, because I didn't have a driver's license or a car at that time, I got around on a little one-and-a-half-horsepower Puch moped bike. I'd pull up to The Alibi on that moped, rev up the tiny engine, and park it right in the middle of those fat boys. The huge bikers watching from the back porch thought it was hilarious. They could've torn me apart, too, mocking their bikes like I was. But I saw myself as a rebel, pushing the envelope, kind of like accepting a dare no one dared me to do, but I did it anyway.

It shows the careless mentality I had—but far more brutal evidence of how gone I really was after the rape came in August when I went out drinking for happy hour on Hillsborough Street in Raleigh. I left the bar stone drunk and got on my moped. I had a Budweiser Long Neck in my pocket (don't ask me why us drunks always carried beer with us), and my motorcycle helmet was on but not properly strapped under my chin. The moped's kickstand was broken, and it was hanging down and banging against the asphalt as I drove, creating little sparks that splashed up and onto the tanks holding the oil and gas. So, despite the beer in my pocket, I tried to hold up the kickstand with my foot so that its bouncing didn't cause the Puch to explode beneath me.

Suddenly, I hit a line of 12 metal mailboxes. Because I was lower to the ground on the moped than I would've been on a standard motorcycle, my head was at just the right height to take out nine of them. My helmet flew off in the process, increasing the damage done to my face.

Down I went, and a friend who happened to be following me in her car saw it all. I couldn't see a thing for the blood gushing from my forehead and my nose, which was no longer positioned where it should be.

What was the first thing I said to her?

"Hide the moped! It is a federal offense to damage mailboxes."

Again, that's the criminal mind at work. I wasn't thinking about my safety, my well-being, or my face. I was more concerned with covering up my high-risk behavior and not getting into trouble. Getting caught may have meant having to slow down my drug use.

She got me into her car, and we went to her apartment. I was still bleeding, the skin was beginning to darken around my eyes, and my nose was on the side of my face, obviously broken. There was a gaping slash on the front of my neck. I wasn't really feeling any pain, though, and I wanted to party. Drinking and drugging had become my only strategy to avoid the pain. Whether that pain was emotional or physical, I just didn't want to feel.

Another friend arrived and insisted on taking me to the hospital. I got stitches for my face and my neck, but they were afraid to fully close up the neck wound for fear of blood draining into my lungs. They couldn't properly reset my nose, either, and they were concerned I had a concussion, so they told me I'd have to stay overnight.

I wasn't having it. As the doctor left to admit me, I left, went to my apartment, showered as best I could, changed clothes, and then did what I planned to do all along. Party.

My actions made all the sense in the world to me. That was my life after the rape.

When the memories of the rape began to return 13 years later, they came slowly in flashbacks, like quick movie clips with no start or end. I remember looking into a mirror and seeing everyone but me. That is called disassociation, and I did it because I wanted to survive. That's very common to trauma. I'd wake up in the middle of the night sitting straight up in bed sweating, and it was like it was happening again, but I never saw me in the mirror until several months into the flashbacks. Then I realized it *was* me, and it was horrible. Later, though, I got a flashback showing how I fought back against my attackers, and that gave me some comfort.

* * *

After those terrible six months hidden away in my apartment, I was determined to go about my business as if everything was okay. I did notice a shift in my personality where, if someone else was getting bullied, I had no problem standing up for them and defending them. It wasn't just that I didn't want them to be victimized, but I had so much rage within me. I cared about others even though I didn't care about myself. I think it was my way of fighting back.

Another thing that happened was I started having sex with men—a lot of sex. I had lost everything, so my previous commitment to virginity just didn't matter any longer. I went on the pill, and with the exception of the occasional drug or alcohol binge where I forgot it for a day or two, I took it faithfully. There was no intimacy about sex. It was just the act. Part of it was that I wanted to use men before they could use me. There were guys that would have been interested in a relationship, but I was not going to let that happen. That would have required some vulnerability. Of course, I wasn't aware of any of this at the time. All I knew was that I used sex as an escape, as a way *not* to feel, and warm bodies worked, at least for a while.

I maintained a life of sex and substance abuse before and after my twenty-first birthday in November. The following year, just after turning 22, I moved to Florida with a friend from high school. She and I had talked about going there together after she graduated from East Carolina University. We chose the destination, Sarasota, by getting out a map and playing a drunken game of pin the tail on the donkey. It was just that random, but it turned out to be one of the first positive things to happen in my life since I left Louisburg. We found an apartment not far from the beach, and I established a routine, getting up early to hit the sand and water, working at night, and playing on a bar softball team. It felt good to be away from North Carolina, and while I still drank and did drugs, I did stop firing dope, at least for a while. Even then, I knew I was going to die if I didn't do something, and I actually tried to do something good for myself. It was a bit of a step forward in a life that had been going in retreat, especially after the rape.

I remained in Florida with my friend until just before my twenty-third birthday. That's when we both decided we were homesick. I missed the changes in the seasons, and during the tropical summers of Florida, the sand got so hot I couldn't even walk on it. I loved the beach, but I didn't like that at all. We both packed up and moved back to Sanford. I rented an old house with four other girls, but I stayed with my parents a lot, too. Really, the house was just a place to party, and I spent most of the week in my old bedroom at home. I didn't place much emotional meaning to being there, though. I still did what I wanted to do. I was pretty strong willed. Strong willed on the outside, but as broken as ever on the inside.

I waited tables at a pretty nice restaurant in Sanford, got another job with a friend managing his office, and I started playing softball again. But I was still partying hard core. I didn't drink or use when I was at my parent's home. I did all of that at the house or elsewhere. My mother and father were retired. He was playing golf every day. She played golf and bridge, and they were both socially active. My interaction with them was normal. I'm pretty sure my mother knew I was drinking much more than I should, but not to the extent that I was spiraling out of control. She tried unsuccessfully to get me to realize what I was doing, to no avail.

I didn't communicate at all with my sisters. Mother talked to them on a regular basis, but I was pretty much out of their lives.

While I wasn't shooting up coke like I had been, I was still drinking and using cocaine. I even started selling it for the first time. I learned it was less expensive to have your own drugs when you're selling because you're able to keep a stash for yourself. I would've had whatever I wanted to use and been able to make plenty of money—if I wasn't an addict. But the amount of cocaine I was using was so out of control I actually *lost* money. If you use dope, you'll never be a profitable drug dealer. Generally, I wasn't afraid of getting caught. I was buying from a "big" supplier, but I wasn't one of the big people in the chain. I was downright teeny tiny.

As 1984 began, I was making okay money in my jobs, but every bit of it was going into drugs and alcohol. I lived for the party. As before, despite all of my issues, I was someone people liked being around. I was a happy-go-lucky person. More unusual, the cocaine helped me to not have blackouts, and I was a nicer person when I was doping. It felt like I was having fun, and that allowed me to not feel anything negative. I felt more lovable and less alone.

I also started seeing the on-again, off-again boyfriend, but we were really nothing more than using buddies. I had so many problems with commitment—with others loving me—that our relationship was never healthy, and I was still so traumatized that he had to be really broken to even try to be with me. I think we wanted what everybody hopes for: a good marriage with your best friend forever, having kids, the picket fence, all of that. The fantasy. But we were both so unhealthy, neither one of us was capable of making that fantasy a reality. At least that's my perspective. I can't tell you his.

That didn't stop us, though, from having sex, and it was one night, sitting on a barstool suddenly so sick that I couldn't drink, that I realized something devastating had happened.

I'd always wanted to have children in spite of the abuse, the neglect, and everything else that I had been through to that point. But when that sickness caused me to check and confirm that I was pregnant, I also knew there was no way I could possibly have the child I was carrying. I was about three months along, and I had been doing drugs and drinking the entire time. There was no way that baby had a chance.

I truly did not feel then that I had another choice, but I will never forget the self-hatred that consumed me as I considered ending the pregnancy. I was raised Catholic. Every fiber in my body was convinced I had already fallen into heavy duty sin. There would be no redemption for me or my unborn child, and there was no way I could tell my parents.

One morning in April 1984, a friend accompanied me to the clinic in Fayetteville, North Carolina.

When I had the abortion, it was kind of like I left my body. The disassociation was a way to protect myself. But I will never forget the sound—the sound of hearing suction, then something heavy hitting something, then more suction.

The "something heavy" was undoubtedly the sound of my unborn child, dead, being thrown away.

It was horrible. Even today, the sound of suction, like you'd hear when seeing a dentist, can take me right back to the cold, sterile clinic room.

Somehow, I know it was a boy. When I talk to men today who are the same age my son would've been had he lived, I wonder, *What would he have looked like?* It doesn't happen as often as it used to when I was younger, but it's still there. From a psychological standpoint, it's all part of accepting what I did. From a spiritual perspective, it makes me aware God is still working on me, and that as He has forgiven me for the abortion, I also have to forgive myself.

But none of that makes it any less painful.

From the clinic, my friend and I went directly to a bar to get lunch and have some beer. We drank *hard* for several hours and then got some more beer for the 30-minute ride home. I kept thinking, *I did this. It was me.* But I didn't want to know that. I wanted—needed—to forget. I didn't care what happened to me. I no longer cared about anything. I didn't feel I was going to live long anyway.

For me, it was over. The abortion represented not just the end of my pregnancy, but of my own life. This was a decision I had made, and the first trauma that I brought on myself. I alone was responsible—and that made it worse than anything else I had done or anything that had been done to me. At that time, I didn't see my choices to do drugs and alcohol as trauma causing. Before this, all the trauma I had experienced had been out of my control at the hands of other people. This was different.

When we got back from Fayetteville, I took a quick shower and went right back out. After all, I knew I wasn't going to get sick anymore, so I might as well party. And I did just about everything I could do except have sex with anyone. That night, sex was the last thing I wanted to do.

When I told my boyfriend about the abortion the next day, that was it. We broke up, and I never thought I'd see him again. That only reinforced the sense that I was bad.

Unlovable.

Unwanted.

Unworthy.

In the months that followed, I made sure I stayed good and partied up. I had to numb myself so that I wouldn't have to deal with what I had done. I didn't even want to think about it. I began having sex, more than ever before, but each time I did, I lost a piece of myself. I was using them, and they were using me. I told myself I wanted to have sex, but it wasn't about *wanting* at all. The alcohol lowered my inhibitions, and my traumas made it effortless to give in. There were many times I'd wake up the next morning and want to cut my arm off because it was under someone lying next to me, and I didn't want to have anything to do with them. Heck, most of the time I couldn't even remember their names. After you're a victim of sexual assault, you typically either abstain completely or become promiscuous. This was not a conscious choice. But I did not want a relationship. Gosh, no! I couldn't tolerate the thought of anyone caring about me. I couldn't even look at myself in the mirror. It wouldn't be until much later that I'd learn you can't love anyone else unless you love yourself first.

I hated me—and I'd continue doing so until many years later when I had therapy for both my sexuality and the abortion.

* * *

In August, I was in Wilmington, North Carolina, about two-and-a-half hours from Sanford, for a weekend softball tournament. We were partying it up Saturday by the pool at the hotel after playing ball all day long, and all of us were drinking, even the coach. It was about midnight when a friend of the team who lived near my parents arrived from Sanford to watch Sunday's games.

She came right up to me. "Your mother wants you to come directly home tomorrow after the tournament."

I was pretty snockered up, but not so much that I didn't realize how unusual that was. My mother had never said anything similar to that before, and certainly wouldn't do so through a messenger when she could've called me herself. I knew something was up.

"What *aren't* you telling me?" I questioned. "My mother has never—"

She interrupted, clearly nervous, and repeated, "She just wants you to come directly home right after the tournament tomorrow."

I went right up to my room and called my mother.

She told me Mary Virginia was dead.

I just fell out. I went into the bathroom and closed the door. It hit me like somebody had punched me in the gut.

In my shock, I must've hung up on my mother because I remember calling her back. She was upset but not crying. That was just like her. "What happened?" I asked, suspecting the worst but not wanting to believe it.

"You know Mary had heart problems and had a quadruple bypass," mom explained, her voice shaking. "They were trying her on different meds, and apparently, she had a heart attack."

Instantly, I suspected that wasn't really what happened.

"You don't have to come home until after the tournament," she added.

Not come home? I thought. *Hell, how in the world am I gonna do that?* It was a harsh indication of just how avoidant my family had become—and perhaps of their expectations of me.

I returned to the friend who had come late, and she agreed to drive me home, right then and there. I left my car behind to be brought back later by one of the other girls on the team. The drive was surreal, as though time itself had stood still—and the more I thought about my sister's death, the more I believed it could not have happened the way mother said it did.

When I got home, even though I'd played softball all day and was a mess, I didn't take a shower. Instead, the instant I arrived home, we left for the Chesapeake Bay, where Mary Virginia had lived with her husband, and went directly to the funeral home where the visitation was already underway. During the drive, mother said Mary Virginia's husband wanted to have her body cremated right away, allegedly because of how she looked when she died, but mother had to talk him out of it. She told him there was no way he could do that to us, her family, before we got to see her. That raised my suspicions even further.

By the time we got there, it was early Sunday afternoon. Mary Virginia's children, Joyce, Willie, and Robbie were there. Joyce, who was almost two years younger than me, was pregnant with what would've been my sister's first grandchild. Joyce wanted to stay in the back. She did not want to see her mother in the casket.

But I did. I *had* to. I walked up, and when I looked at her body, I immediately noticed bruising around her face and all up and down her arms and on her hands. She looked very forced in her posturing, like rigor mortis had set in too soon.

It was odd. Very odd.

And that's when I knew, I just *knew*, this was no heart attack.

It was a suicide.

Mary Virginia had overdosed.

The fact that it wasn't officially confirmed until after her autopsy much later didn't change anything. Mary Virginia's past spoke for itself. She'd tried to end it all many times before. Not because she ever intended to actually die. I don't believe that. Every time, it was a desperate cry for attention. For help. But who could possibly help her? I couldn't, not in the state I was in. Apparently, her husband couldn't either. He was with Mary Virginia when it happened, and he evidently knew that was what was going on, but even after everything that had happened before, he didn't think it was serious enough to respond—not until it was too late. When he finally tried to do something to revive her, his actions caused the bruising on her body.

I hadn't had any sleep, so it was all a blur, like I was moving in slow motion. That night at the hotel, I spoke to all three of Mary Virginia's kids, and we all agreed their mother had overdosed.

The next morning, we went to the Catholic church that was to oversee Mary Virginia's memorial service. By this point my father was overwhelmed. I've never seen my dad cry like that. Mom still wouldn't shed a tear. My sister's body had just been unloaded from the hearse, and we were lining up to go in behind the casket, when the priest came out to see my parents.

What I heard him say next turned me seven shades of crazy.

"We received word that your daughter committed suicide. We can't allow her memorial to be done from this church."

There we were, in this quaint, very *Catholic* church that was considered to be on holy ground, and they weren't going to conduct the service?

I couldn't believe they would do that to my parents, and I certainly wasn't going to stand for it. I was close to five-foot-ten at the time, and he was a little sawed-off fella. I was angry, and I stood erect in front of him, towering over him, and stared straight down into his eyes.

"I have no idea where you got your information," I told him, "but as far as *we* know as her family, she died of heart-related issues. So, unless you have something official, and you *don't,* my sister *is* going to have her service from this church."

I was stern. I was succinct. That tiny whippersnapper of a priest knew there would be hell to pay from me if he challenged us.

He relented, the memorial took place, and we all went home. After the autopsy was done at the state capital, Mary Virginia's ashes were released to her husband—but burning anger smoldered in my heart. When someone grieves, they pass through five stages: denial, anger, bargaining, depression, and acceptance, but it isn't always a stepwise progression. Back then, I went straight to anger and stayed there for a while. I never fully grieved her death. I was drinking and drugging, which only complicated my grief. It was a convoluted time. I just got pissed off at her for being so selfish and doing this crap. Today, though, I have total empathy for her. Because I am healed, I can see the situation more clearly. She suffered her whole life from debilitating depression. I loved her dearly because she was the primary caretaker for me when my mother had postpartum depression after I was born. Mary Virginia was gifted, extremely artistic, and could've easily been a concert pianist. She used chalk, paint, and charcoal to create beautiful art. She'd done drawings of both me and of our mother. I received those after her death. I still have them today. It is the spitting image of me. She did a silhouette. I was probably five or six years old when she drew it.

The month after her suicide was a blur. I was drinking heavily and doing cocaine while playing ball on the weekends. I was on a traveling team that was part of the United States Slowpitch Softball Association and competed against other teams all along the eastern seaboard.

It was nothing for me to use and drink all night and go to that ball field at the crack of dawn and play ball, beer in hand as I walked to the dugout to get ready for the game. I played in 100-degree heat without any sleep and had alcohol seeping out of my pores, and I was still one of the better athletes on the diamond.

My life was beyond insane—and it was only going to get crazier.

Chapter 3

Bottoming Out

"Who shall separate us from the love of Christ? Shall trouble or hardship or persecution or famine or nakedness or danger or sword? As it is written: 'For your sake we face death all day long; we are considered as sheep to be slaughtered.' ... For I am convinced that neither death nor life, neither angels nor demons, neither the present nor the future, nor any powers, neither height nor depth, nor anything else in all creation, will be able to separate us from the love of God that is in Christ Jesus our Lord."

Romans 8:35-36, 38-39

had always been around lesbians. As a college athlete, I had homosexual friends and was around the homosexual lifestyle—and it didn't blow my skirt up one way or the other, even when many of those lesbian friends found me attractive. Since that early expression of same sex attraction with Colleen, I'd been attracted to both boys and girls, but I had never acted on it with a female.

Then there was one woman I had come to really like. I knew her from high school where we played basketball on the same team, and though we weren't close back then, I knew she was a lesbian. She was a year or so younger than me, and we started hanging out together again on a women's league volleyball team.

She was kind. She was fun and sweet. She was pretty.

When we first became sexually intimate in November after a night out partying, she didn't make the move. I did. Yet my actions weren't an intentional decision to fulfill the same sex attraction I'd first felt as a youngster and officially become a lesbian. They *were* an intentional choice to have an intimate connection with another human being. I had started to become so numb to men, and I was beginning to associate men with so much of the pain I tried to avoid, especially the trauma from the assault.

It seemed like a different choice might be best. Different sounded good. I wanted to be close with someone. I was very empty. I wanted to be connected. To feel like I belonged. To feel like I was wanted.

She provided that connection.

While our relationship would be brief, lasting just four months, it easily became the most intense relationship I'd ever had to that point.

Until then, including the young man with whom I became pregnant, the truth was I'd only had one serious relationship—and it was with my addiction. My addiction was my best friend/boyfriend-girlfriend all rolled up into one. It was all I had. It was my only constant. It was *the* connection in my life. But I couldn't *feel* anything in the throes of my relationship with addiction. It did quite the opposite. It made me numb. After all, that was the point.

With this girl, I was able to feel for the first time. But as I began sharing some of my deepest hurts with her, wounds I'd never shared with anyone else, the weight of those hurts began to push her away. She started pulling away. In a drunken stupor, I slept with her brother and lied to her about it. She moved away in June, and with that, our relationship fizzled out and died.

I was pretty much devastated. I attempted and had, for a short time, a real physical, emotional connection with another human being. When it was over, I suddenly believed I couldn't do anything right. I couldn't handle my addiction right. I couldn't handle a relationship right. I couldn't handle anything right.

Abuse had killed my childhood innocence.

Rape had killed my commitment to remain pure.

My unborn child had died, and part of me with him.

Mary Virginia had died.

My first real relationship with a person had died.

My addiction was making sure I was dying.

I was a failure through and through.

Oddly, I had stopped shooting drugs by then and had switched mostly to alcohol, though I still dabbled with snorting cocaine or popping speed every once in a while. I wasn't dealing, either. There was just something about intravenous drug use that made me realize it was going to kill me if I didn't stop. Putting it directly into your bloodstream like that, your heart feels all of it. Yet while my drug use had changed, my alcoholism was getting even worse. My blackouts increased, and I was heavily depressed every day, even if I didn't know it at the time— and I was suicidal. One night I almost tried to kill myself.

The only thing that kept me from doing it, the only saving grace, was the pain my parents went through when Mary Virginia killed herself. I did not want to put them through that again. I simply couldn't.

There was no joy. I was at a real bad point. I don't remember a whole lot about that time. It was so dark. I was teetering on the abyss.

That was late March. A couple of weeks later, I got my second DUI. I was so drunk all I recall about the traffic incident was getting pulled over and put in the backseat of the police car. Then squalling. I begged and pleaded for them to let me go. When I was placed in jail, I raised hell. Anger, rage, and grief poured out of me. It was so bad a woman from another cell yelled, "If you don't shut up, I'm gonna kill you!"

I looked at one of the women in my cell. "What the hell is that woman in here for?" I asked.

I instantly wished I hadn't. "She is in here for murder."

Because of its strict laws, North Carolina was not the place to have a DUI. Even though it had been a while since the first DUI, it was my second in a seven-year period, so my parents had to hire an attorney. In the end, I was convicted of the DUI, placed on probation, and I had to go to jail every weekend for two months starting in June: in at 6:00 p.m. every Friday and out at 6:00 a.m. every Monday. I played ball during the week, and I got a pretty good routine down when I was in jail. It didn't have air conditioning, so because I was there in the heat of the summer, I learned what to wear to be warm enough in the evenings and cool enough during the days. I took in stuff to read, and I wrote letters. I'd always been able to get along with people, and that helped me with the other inmates. There was one girl, I think she was in for grand theft auto, who was in my bunk cell the duration of my stay in jail. I brought her cigarettes, so we were buddies. But the others weren't to be messed with, I can tell you that. I wasn't in there with just a bunch of drunks.

The cell I was in was an open space that had two bunks in each enclosure, and each cell contained 12 women. It wasn't fun. I learned to sleep with one eye open. But I could handle myself. I was an athlete, slim and muscular, and I kept a posture about me that made it so that people knew not to mess with me. The worst thing for me was wondering what would happen if the place caught on fire. You don't want to think about that while you are locked in a jail cell, but that's where my mind went whenever I tried to rest.

Just before the end of my sentence in August, I went back to Wilmington with my softball team. My coach promised to have me back in time on Friday, but we played some extra games and were late getting back. Imagine the irony of me banging on the doors of the jail for them to let me in, but they wouldn't do it because I was late. I ended up having to go back to court, and even though the tardiness wasn't my fault, the judge threw the book at me. He added on to my sentence, requiring me to serve Monday through Friday 6:00 p.m. to 6:00 a.m. for the next four weeks.

Throughout it all, I had to regularly check in with a probation officer, Mary Dawkins, who years later would end up saving my life. I also had to do community service working at the courthouse in the clerk's office. I believe I was placed in the clerk's office because I was from a good all-American family. I wasn't out somewhere picking up trash, though I really should've been. The community service at the courthouse was fitting since I began going to school in the fall to study law. It was at a little community college in Sanford, and I took a full load of classes in addition to pursuing a minor in criminal justice. Unfortunately, the last two weeks of my extended jail time overlapped with the start of school, and while I was allowed to leave the jail during the day to attend classes, my mother had to pick me up from the jail and drop me back off each day. I hated that. I felt bad that she had to do all this running around, just to help me. She absolutely loved me and thought I was better than sliced bread, regardless of my bad choices and behaviors—and yet, there she was, having to pick up her baby daughter out of jail. It just wasn't good.

Finally, that awful stint in jail ended, and I focused on my classes at the community college. For the next semester, I took courses designed to allow me to finish the undergraduate studies that I'd started at Louisburg. That included a psychology class that I found I really loved, and I even tutored a couple of students in the subject. The schooling gave me something to do—which was good because, otherwise, I was like a zombie. I didn't really venture out to make friends at school, which was so unlike me. As far as I was concerned, life sucked. The passionate love-to-laugh person I had been was long gone. My vicious sense of humor had lost its edge. I lived with my parents, so my mom continued driving me to school and picking me up because I didn't have a driver's license. That confirmed my low self-esteem and just how low I had sunk. But I still partied on the weekends when my friends took me away with them.

I succeeded well enough in community college to be able to leave there and begin attending Campbell University in Buies Creek, North Carolina in January 1986, where my enjoyment of that first psychology class inspired me to pursue a bachelor's degree in psychology at Campbell. I couldn't get enough of the subject. However, I definitely had a Dr. Jekyll and Mr. Hyde personality. At school I was one way. Away from there with my friends, we'd start drinking on Friday and drank solid straight through the weekend without sleeping. I was a binge drinker who experienced blackouts.

I was scheduled to graduate with my degree in May 1987, but we had a huge snowstorm blow through in April, during which I went on a bender and didn't come home, or back to school, for an entire week. I pretty much self-sabotaged, and it cost me. I couldn't catch up in time. But that didn't keep me from lying to my parents and telling them I did get the degree when I really hadn't. I didn't want to disappoint them.

It was around that same time that I avoided a third DUI. I finally had my driver's license again, and I was driving with a friend when I lost control and rolled the car on a sandy road near the university. Of course, I had been drinking, so after unlatching my friend from the passenger seat (we were both upside down but not injured), I left her and the car, ran, and hid myself in a dorm building on campus until I sobered up. Then I called the state trooper's office and turned myself in—and even though they knew I deserved a DUI, they couldn't give me one because they couldn't prove I'd been drinking when the rollover happened.

Incredibly, it'd be another three years before I'd find myself in that situation again.

* * *

The summer of 1987, I began working at a warehouse being run by my softball coach. I oversaw a returns program for a distribution center. It was decent work making okay money, and I kept up with it nicely even as my drinking worsened. My intolerance for alcohol had built to the point that I was having blackouts almost every time I drank. It didn't matter if it was four beers or 24, out I went—and that started to put a strain on my friendships because when I blacked out, I was obnoxious and full of rage. I liked people and thought I had a shun-proof personality, but people began to not even want to hang out with me. That made me feel lonelier and more distant than ever. I had always been seen as the "fun" girl, but everything had changed. It was a bad time.

At the end of that year, I moved out of my parent's house, and with their help, bought a brand-new single wide mobile home and moved it onto a little piece of land in Lee County, North Carolina. It was the first time I had owned a home. My roommate was a teammate and drinking buddy. She and I had a relationship that was neither sexual attraction nor love, but a strange coexistence that I'm not even sure I'd characterize today as a relationship, although others probably did at the time. She lived in one part of the trailer, and I lived in the other. I loved and cared about her, but I was not *in* love with her, though I think she was in love with me. I was in an alcoholic fog. I was having depressive episodes, and I needed to be around someone, anyone. More than that, I needed to feel connected to someone.

Throughout the next five years, she and I lived together until I sold that home in 1993, but we were roommates and nothing more. I simply wasn't capable of anything more than that with her or anyone else. In the midst of drinking and playing softball, I took another job at a different warehouse where I was quickly promoted from pulling orders to doing direct sales and managing export shipments. I excelled as an employee and was even exhibiting leadership capabilities, but because I was a binge drinker—a chronic alcoholic—I never fully recognized or appreciated who I was or what I was capable of achieving when I wasn't drinking.

Then came the night in October 1990 when everything started to change. Just after a coed softball tournament, I got my roommate, and we went to get some fast food. I was driving, and we'd both been drinking, but, ironically, I was not in a blackout. I pulled out of the restaurant drive-thru without paying attention and ran through a red light—right in front of a watching police officer.

When he pulled us over, I had an ingenious idea. Drunk people think they are so smart. I thought if I rolled up the window and locked the doors, he couldn't do anything. I just wouldn't let him in the car.

That'd do it.

Uh, no.

He told me if I didn't roll down the window, he'd have my car towed—with me in it—and I'd go to jail.

Well, I guess I can't run from this one, can I?

I was detained overnight and released with a January court date. My roommate picked me up, and as she drove me home, I knew the third DUI meant I was likely in big trouble.

For the first time ever, I made a promise to myself that I was going to stop drinking. At the advice of a lawyer, who was also a past party buddy, I decided in November to get a mental health assessment. The idea was that getting the assessment would make me look good to the judge when I went to court. It was conducted at the same mental health center where I did my internship while going to school at Campbell. Talk about a hit to my pride. I had gone from a worker to, in some sense, a patient.

I went in there dressed to the nines. I had on a nice business suit complete with pantyhose and pumps, and I wore glasses. I felt like I was in drag, and I was, in that I was portraying myself as something that I wasn't. It was all about appearance. I was even carrying a leather notebook filled with the notes I knew I'd need for the assessment. After all, I used to give the very same assessment to patients during my past internship.

As I walked in, I just hoped I didn't see anyone that knew me from my internship. I was so uptight. After all, this was my third DUI. A first DUI is one thing, maybe a second, but a third? I took a seat in the evaluator's office. He cut to the chase. "Miss Lynch, do you think that's a problem, three DUI's?"

I couldn't lie anymore. I took off my glasses, tried to hold my composure, and responded, "Yes, sir. It is a problem." He didn't know that was the first time I'd ever admitted to having an alcohol problem to another human being. The façade I'd built up for so long was beginning to crack, if just a little.

"Okay," he said, "we can work with that." He then recommended some educational classes I could take on alcoholism. I signed up for all of them, not out of an earnest desire to learn about alcoholism, but because I wanted to put my best foot forward for the judge. Still, I had admitted that I had a problem out loud, a radical change for someone who had protected her addiction all of her life.

So, I attended the classes, and I stayed away from alcohol—until New Year's Eve, 1990. That's when I didn't just fall off the wagon. I plummeted from that thing. I drank a boatload that night: beer, some shots, and I even took some speed. And, because I had broken my promise to myself, I became suicidal, so much so my roommate got the pistol that I kept in my nightstand and took it out of my room.

But the crazy thing was, I couldn't get drunk. No matter how much I drank, I could not numb this amount of pain. Maybe it was the two months of abstinence. Perhaps it was the sense of guilt and failure I hoped the alcohol would drown. Whatever it was, that binge only made me so ill it took me days to recover. After that, I stayed dry, but I started stressing myself out so bad about the court date that sleep was next to impossible. I was worried sick, and I became so distraught at times that my roommate was concerned I might again consider killing myself. Ultimately, Mary Virginia's memory and my determination not to do that to my parents prevented me from suicide. But, boy, it didn't prevent the pain.

Question was, how long could that continue?

* * *

On January 6, 1991, I began attending Alcoholics Anonymous (AA) in Raleigh. I went 60 miles away from where I lived so that no one would know me. That first day in AA, I went in and acted like I had my crap together. I don't know what I was trying to hide. My mindset was, *Something is wrong with them, but I'm fine.*

I took a seat in one of the plastic chairs, which had been arranged in a circle in the middle of what looked like a classroom. It was on the second floor of an office building with windows on one side of the brightly lit room.

There were probably 10 women there. Of course, I knew one of them, and she also recognized me. *So much for staying incognito.*

The group leader, who was positioned directly across from me, asked, "Does anybody want to read?"

I grabbed the first thing I saw in front of me, a paper titled "How it Works." I'd later learn it was from Chapter Five of the "Big Book," the basic text for Alcoholics Anonymous. I read aloud a segment that said, "Remember that we deal with alcohol—cunning, baffling, powerful! Without help it is too much for us. But there is One who has all power—that One is God."

I could hardly believe what was coming out of my mouth. A few lines later, I came to their steps of recovery.

1. We admitted we were powerless over alcohol—that our lives had become unmanageable.
2. Came to believe that a Power greater than ourselves could restore us to sanity.
3. Made a decision to turn our will and our lives over to the care of God as we understood Him.
4. Made a searching and fearless moral inventory of ourselves.
5. Admitted to God, to ourselves, and to another human being the exact nature of our wrongs.
6. Were entirely ready to have God remove all these defects of character.
7. Humbly asked Him to remove our shortcomings.
8. Made a list of all persons we had harmed, and became willing to make amends to them all.
9. Made direct amends to such people wherever possible, except when to do so would injure them or others.

10. Continued to take personal inventory and when we were wrong promptly admitted it.
11. Sought through prayer and meditation to improve our conscious contact with God as we understood Him, praying only for knowledge of His will for us and the power to carry that out.
12. Having had a spiritual awakening as the result of these steps, we tried to carry this message to alcoholics, and to practice these principles in all our affairs.

I put the paper down, and as I reflected on what I had just read aloud, I was so nervous I could barely hold in the bile scorching my throat.

When I saw God first mentioned in the third step, my initial thought was, *I am going to drink again.* My knowledge of God was so poor, so broken, it was almost impossible to think I could turn my will and my life over to His care. God, as I understood Him then, was the one I had been raised with: a hellfire and brimstone, punishing, guilt-slinging God.

AA was reintroducing me to God. The true God. But was I going to miss Him because of who I thought He was?

Confused, I based my recovery on the group as my higher power. The group itself was filled with like-minded people, and as I attended more meetings, I began remembering some of them from nights I'd gone out partying. I certainly hadn't cared what they thought of me when I was out at the bar showing my tail. But over subsequent meetings, I'd go in five minutes late and leave five minutes early in hopes they wouldn't notice me. For sure, I did not want to speak to anyone.

Yet as I played my futile hiding game, it was clear that none of them were drinking any longer. *How are they not drinking?* I wondered. I'd later learn they smoked and drank a lot of coffee, and that there were some emotionally unhealthy folks in there who needed to work on some other things besides putting the plug in the jug.

But they were sober. That was incredible to me.

I didn't share anything that first day. I wouldn't have known what to say. At the end of the meeting, someone mentioned that chips, these round, coin-sized sobriety tokens, were going to be offered to everyone, and that sponsors were available. Of course, my mind first went to athletic sponsorships (not at all what AA had in mind), and when I got my chip, it was a white one that symbolized the motto, "surrender to win." It indicated that I had admitted I was an alcoholic and that I wanted to walk a new life.

I had never surrendered to anything in my life before then because I was hardheaded. I didn't know any other way to live, so I kept going. Of course, I should have surrendered when I was raped, or when I almost lost my life on the moped, or when I got my second DUI. I surely should've surrendered when I lost my sister to suicide. But I had always been taught as a kid and as an athlete to never give up. That was what surrender felt like to me. Giving up.

You never surrender. That was my mantra, one that also fed the denial that goes along with addiction.

Once I took the chip, I instantly wanted to give it back, knowing what it meant. But I already had it in my hand, and I was trying to look cool, trying to preserve that image, so I kept it. I did leave right away, though. In addition to the emotions churning within me, emotions that made me very uncomfortable, I also felt awkward, as if I couldn't talk to anyone. I thought being able to talk and have friends was equated with drinking alcohol. I didn't know what to do.

That was on a Sunday. Two days later, I went to an AA meeting featuring a speaker. When he was first introduced, a fifty-something former CEO of a large company, I felt I had nothing in common with him. Then he started talking about having blackouts, of not knowing what he did but looking at people's faces, and of seeing how disgusted they were with him.

Oh, my God, I thought. *He's talking about me!*

All those feelings from Sunday suddenly resurfaced, and I am telling you, I was freaking out. Alcoholics don't talk about their feelings, yet there he was, up there talking about all these feelings he had, and it was making my skin crawl. I felt like he was telling *my* story, even if we didn't have anything in common other than alcoholism. He ended up being a drunk underneath the bridge. Alcoholism took away his relationships, his marriage, his children, all his financial wealth, *everything.* It made my stomach quiver with nausea.

I couldn't get out of there fast enough. But it had me hooked because he was telling stuff I would never have told anyone else in private, much less from a podium. I was going to take my stuff to my grave.

He had been sober for years, which I thought was an absolute miracle.

If he could do it, I thought, *maybe I can, too.*

That speaker spoke of hope! That was God working in my life even then.

* * *

A couple of weeks after hearing the AA speaker, my court date arrived, and my parents drove me to the courthouse. I remember being all dressed up and walking into the courtroom with my whole body wet with sweat. I may have looked okay on the outside, but I was shaking uncontrollably on the inside.

The hearing was brief. Mary Dawkins, my probation officer, said, "Your honor, her parents are quite capable of paying these fines, and if she is not held more accountable for this, this pattern of behavior is going to continue." I was so angry with her for saying that. So were my parents. But it was exactly what I needed. She did it, no matter how we felt, because she knew it was in my best interest. I was convicted and sentenced. Later, when I was almost one year sober, I wrote Mary a letter telling her how much I appreciated her for doing what she did. I believe it literally saved my life.

I had to serve four consecutive weekends in the county jail. I lost my driver's license for a year. I was also placed on probation, but it could've been way worse. I was lucky I wasn't going to prison. Still, not long after the sentencing, I lost my job. Ironically, it had nothing to do with my drinking. I had a good salary, and it was a layoff to cut back on expenses. You talk about depressed? I was unemployed, and it wasn't even of my own doing, and I had to go to jail. The timing was terrible.

I started drawing unemployment leading up to my first weekend behind bars in February. Despite my AA experiences, I thought I had literally bottomed out. The elevator of my life only went down. I could get off at any floor, any bottom along the way—abuse, rejection, rape, suicide, you name it—but it only went down. The last bottom was death, and I was knocking on death's door.

I also knew that if I ever drank again, I was either going to kill myself, kill someone else, or both.

I was as low as I could get without actually being dead.

Chapter 4

Discovering Hope and a Calling

*"For we are God's handiwork, created in Christ Jesus to do
good works, which God prepared in advance for us to do ...
remember that at that time you were separate from Christ,
excluded from citizenship in Israel and foreigners to the
covenants of the promise, without hope and without God in
the world. But now in Christ Jesus you who once were far
away have been brought near by the blood of Christ."*

Ephesians 2:10, 12-13

As the cell door clanged shut, I thought my life
was over.

I truly didn't want it to be. Sure, I loathed
myself. I absolutely hated who I had become. I couldn't
even look at myself in the mirror. But after everything I

had been through, it was no wonder I felt like I was the scum of the earth.

Lonely.

Unwanted.

Unworthy.

Helpless.

Hopeless.

Yet even then, I still knew there was someone deep down within me who truly cared about people. Even loved them, but could I really love people without pushing them away? Could I be vulnerable in the way a relationship required?

I plopped down onto the bunk in the cell, all by myself with no one to call, and no one at whom to point a finger. Addicts love to pass blame, but there was no one left to blame.

I did do one thing, though.

"God. Please help me."

It was a simple plea, one I had never made before, even in my most horrific moments. But I did in that moment, inspired by what I had seen and heard at Alcoholics Anonymous, and it was sincere. My surrender chip from AA was still in my pocket.

I was acknowledging I had a problem.

Even more, I was acknowledging it to Him.

At that moment, the Lord responded, not with an audible voice or a vision of some 50-foot-tall Jesus basking in heaven's light, but with a feeling.

A sense.

I didn't know what that meant or how it was going to play out in my life. But suddenly, shockingly, I knew in my heart I was going to be okay.

At age 31, propelled by that tiny act of faith and His response, I was instantly spiritually and mentally released from the bondage of alcoholism.

I knew it was going to be different, and what I sensed had to be the presence of God.

It just *had* to be—because I had hope.

I'd never had hope before.

From then on, that hope became the foundation for my recovery as I sought to seek God and push myself to get better.

*   *   *

As I served the four weekends in jail, I began going to AA meetings in Sanford twice a day. I'd been laid off from work, and that was a God thing. I needed to be actively involved in the recovery process. I went to a meeting at noon and another one at 8:00 p.m. We all called the AA building "319 Moore St." after its street address. We had our own clubhouse. I began to learn not to drink one day at a time and to deal with life on *life's* terms. I also started discovering how to *feel* feelings. I had cut off feelings of grief and emotional pain for years, but I had to experience those feelings, and then deal with them, without alcohol. It was a tall order.

The AA meetings became a safe place where I was able to acknowledge that alcohol was just a symptom of the real problem: me. The real problem was Jeannie. I had a "broken coper" so when things started to happen to me, I wanted to escape. Somewhere along the line, when life started to be unfair and I didn't know how to deal with it, I tried to fix my broken coper with alcohol. It helped me to survive for a while, but it had turned its back on me. So, I had to learn to deal with Jeannie. Yet the longer I stayed sober, the more my past bubbled up to the surface. I hadn't dealt with anything in over 21 years, not since I had first started drinking at age 10. Therefore, my emotional health and development was stunted. I was a 31-year-old woman with the emotional mentality of a 10-year-old. I was an adult woman who didn't have a clue about relationships, boundaries—anything.

It was also in those meetings that I learned there were other people just like me. I was not unique, nor was I the scum of the earth, even though I often felt like it. The horrible things that I'd done, or that had happened to me, had been done by, or had happened to, others as well, yet they weren't drinking. You can't con a con, though, so I picked out the people who were working the program, the winners, and I hung with them. I knew they were the ones who were going to teach me how to be sober and stay that way. I was competitive, an edge from the athlete in me, so when I set my mind to get sober, come hell or high water, I was going to do it.

Near the end of February, I picked an AA sponsor who was about two years sober. She was married and a little younger than me. In AA, you are supposed to call your sponsor every day, and there were times I would rather have had every tooth in my mouth pulled than to make that call. That is the honest to God truth. It was as if the phone weighed ten thousand pounds. I mean, I was planning to go to a priest and confess all of my stuff— not because I was a practicing Catholic, but I sure as hell wasn't going to share it all with just any old human being. As far as I was concerned, my stuff was going with me to the grave. My sponsor didn't put up with my arrogance and my pride, though, and as we talked, I got close with her and her husband, and developed an ever-growing relationship. I began to trust her with my struggles and pain.

That was a huge milestone for me. For the first time, I began to feel accepted, even loved and valued.

My AA group in Sanford consisted of probably 100 or more men and women, including married couples with children. Some of us began having game nights where we played pool and Pictionary, and we had a good time. That was where I learned I could be sober and still have a lot of fun, which is a real worry for addicts. We cut up, and I didn't get locked up. I thought that was a miracle. I began doing service work, too. I was cleaning the clubhouse at least once a month, and I even scrubbed commodes.

In April, I got a sales job in Sanford, which forced me to reduce my AA meetings to once every night, but I kept going and continued working with my sponsor. Shortly after that, I planned a camping trip on the Nantahala River, at a site just outside of Bryson City, North Carolina. I was about six months sober by then, and all of us went, ten women. I actually guided them down the Nantahala in a raft. It had some good rapids, and I felt I was the only one who knew what they were doing. I sat on the back of the raft trying to get the women to paddle correctly, but they didn't do anything right. So, we ended up going down the rapids backward, the very thing we were not supposed to do. Yet not one woman fell out of the boat—except for me. When it hit the first rapid, it shot me up like a bullet. I probably went a good six feet or more up in the air and then back down into the water. I tell you, I got pummeled. We had an absolute ball—and what an analogy it provided of the hard lessons I was learning through my sobriety. The reality of being sober is that sometimes the consequences of old behaviors don't catch up to you until you are doing things correctly—just like going down the rapids backwards. When I was drinking, I cut corners and did everything the easy way. But when I got sober, I had to face the consequences of that. On the rafting trip, I paid the consequence of going backwards by getting thrown. In addition, when I was drinking, I blamed other people or things for my problems and never took any responsibility. When I was sober, I started to take responsibility, but in the raft, I still wanted to blame everyone else. If I had taken the time to teach the women properly, we probably would have gone down the river correctly.

As I continued the AA meetings, I also discovered the Lord wasn't all hellfire and brimstone. I learned that He loved me. It was a massive turning point. I knew Him before, but in a different way than I was learning to know Him now. This time wasn't about rules and the Catholic doctrine. This time it was about my heart, His heart, and His heart for me. It was about relationship.

In that moment, though I'm still not sure how, I had hope of being loved.

Hope of being enough.

*   *   *

It wasn't until December, near the end of the first full year of being sober, that things began to crumble.

It started with Lois Jean's death. My sister passed away two days after Christmas. My mom told me over the phone, and I flew to D.C. for the funeral. Much of my family was already there for the holiday. I had been invited to join them, but I'd chosen not to go. I knew my nephews would be drinking, and I didn't want to be in that environment because of my recovery. As it was, I was so thankful my parents were there and got to spend that Christmas with Lois Jean and her family before she passed away.

Her death was from natural causes, contributed to by her condition. She was down to one lung because of the curvature of her spine and the paralysis, and that lung just gave out. She simply stopped breathing. Lois Jean was 57. Considering her health, it was incredible that she lived that long.

I hadn't seen Lois Jean since summer 1987 when her middle son got married, and even then, we hardly talked because I stayed drunk the whole time. I hadn't really interacted with Lois Jean since leaving for North Carolina. While it was true that I never missed Lois Jean, and while it was also true that I had been hurt by her in several ways as a child and teenager, her death was truly difficult for me because it began a domino effect. I had been drunk or anesthetized for close to 22 years. Now, in my sobriety, I not only felt the loss of Lois Jean's death, but of Mary Virginia's suicide, of the abortion, the violent rape and assault, and of all the other losses or disappointments I had experienced. They all started tumbling in.

Her death became a shock to my psyche—a trigger that sent my mind into a tailspin and subsequent crash I could never have anticipated.

As 1992 began, I started having flashbacks. They were horrific, nightmarish scenes, like short movie clips but with vivid surround sound. These flashbacks woke me up in the middle of the night, and I'd find myself sitting straight up in the middle of my bed, panting and sweating as if I'd been running non-stop for miles.

I saw blood on the walls.

I saw three men.

I could hear the sound of blows hitting flesh.

I could almost sense the feeling of being beaten, but I couldn't see myself in these macabre incidents.

I didn't know it was me. Not yet.

In the meantime, I went to see a clinical psychologist in Raleigh, thinking maybe she could help with everything I was experiencing. That was the first time I discovered that not all therapists are good.

"You just need to cry," she told me.

I looked at her like she had 12 heads. "Woman, if I knew how to cry, I wouldn't be paying you $125 to come in here to learn."

It was so frustrating, and that was my last visit to her. Shortly after that, a friend in AA who was a substance abuse counselor recommended a different therapist, a lady she knew in Raleigh. She was much better than the first therapist, and I started seeing her weekly. It was one night after seeing the therapist that I finally broke down and sobbed all the way from Raleigh to Sanford. When I arrived at the AA meeting I was supposed to attend, I couldn't even go inside because I was just a puddle of tears. I hadn't cried in so long.

Before long, she referred me to a psychiatrist who, in March, diagnosed me with major depressive disorder (recurrent) and post-traumatic stress disorder, or PTSD (chronic).

It was the first time I had been officially diagnosed with mental illness. Looking back today, the diagnoses were important because they let me know that I wasn't going crazy. To realize for the first time that everything I had been feeling, the depression and the trauma, had a name? It was a relief.

At the same time, the flashbacks intensified. In one, I remembered snow and walking out of a trailer feeling the sensation of blood blisters cracking on my face. In another, I looked into a mirror, saw my body standing there in the reflection, and I could see one of the three men standing right behind me—but I could not see my face. I know now that is called disassociation. Then, when I finally realized that it was me who was being raped and beaten, it was as if I was outside of my body. That, too, was disassociation, the only way my brain could process it without driving me mad.

It was terrifying.

Finally, one night while I was on the phone with my sponsor, I told her, for the first time, about what I had seen in the flashbacks—and I shared with her how I was raped and beaten. I'd never told anyone that before. How could I? I didn't have any knowledge of it until then.

It was a repressed memory.

Strangely, I spoke of the rape to my sponsor with absolutely no emotion. I was disconnected from my feelings, relying on her to somehow feel them *for* me.

We hung up, and I went to bed. Later, my sponsor told me she could not stop crying after she got off the phone.

I actually felt bad for her, but I had no feelings for myself about the assault. None whatsoever. Those emotions were literally locked away in my brain, inaccessible.

That surprising confession to my sponsor did not stop my mental torment. The flashbacks continued, and now that I knew that what I was seeing had actually happened to me, it was far more than memories. I was *reliving* it all, going through the assault again and again. It made me angry, though I didn't really know it was anger. I even began having suicidal ideation: concrete thoughts of suicide. I didn't want to overdose. I wouldn't have done that. I certainly would have blown my head off, though. That would be a more certain way to die.

I kept saying to myself, "I just want to evaporate." Fade away. Not be here.

I had another thought.

If this is what being sober is like, I don't want it.

*   *   *

It kept building up throughout the summer until, in August, I had a full-blown panic attack at work. It happened right before lunch. I was at my desk doing sales calls when I got up and suddenly found I could barely walk to my boss's desk just a few steps away from mine.

Out of nowhere, I felt like I was having a heart attack. I started hyperventilating. Tears were coming out of me every which way. I could not make it stop. It was devastating.

My mother had to pick me up. The next day, I was off to a clinic in Roanoke, Alabama operated by my therapist's best friend—and there I stayed, as a patient, for the next 30 days.

That month in Alabama changed my life.

All of our therapy was done in groups of 21-25 individuals who had all kinds of different diagnoses: from PTSD, codependence, depression, and suicide issues to drug and alcohol addiction, sexual abuse and sex addiction, and gambling.

We met daily from 9:00 a.m. to 3:30 p.m. with lunch somewhere in between. During that time we did processing sessions to review what was helpful or not and decide what actions to continue or change, didactic therapy designed to educate addicts about issues, behaviors, and consequences related to their substance use disorders, and experiential therapy using expressive tools and activities such as role playing to re-enact and re-experience past and recent emotional situations.

It was thorough. It was engaging—and I knew, from those initial moments sitting in the group, that I was going to become a therapist. Not only did I have my previous internship experiences to take into account, but I was often chosen in our peer group sessions to be the person to confront my peers because they responded better to a peer than they did to a therapist. My gift began to emerge, and I got to know every single person there on a very personal level. I truly cared about them. It was an incredible experience for me.

I had been placed on Prozac, and my dosage was increased while I was at the clinic, from 20 milligrams to 40, and it was as though somebody had turned on the daggone lights. I don't know how else to explain it. I had been so severely depressed that I felt like I was in a dungeon. Meanwhile, my diagnoses of major depressive disorder and PTSD were successfully addressed in therapy, particularly through role play and letter writing. I experienced a lot of resolution regarding Mary Virginia's suicide. Through the experiential role play, I was able to deal with the emotion from that loss. I was finally able to grieve it for the first time. The rage that was smoldering right beneath the surface was given an escape.

I had two more flashbacks while I was there, and both were tremendously significant. In one, I again saw the blood on the walls of the trailer where I was raped and realized, for the first time, that it was *my* blood. In the second, as one of the men came toward me, I saw myself kick him hard in the testicles while his penis was erect. While that was the act that caused the horrible beating that I endured, it was liberating to know with certainty that I had tried to fight back. That realization made all the difference to me. I was victimized, but I wasn't a helpless victim.

That flashback was actually an answer to prayer—and it brought such healing that I was able to start the process of forgiving the three men who raped me. I was able to forgive God as well. I had always thought He was punishing me for being a bad person, but I was beginning to realize that wasn't true. In addition, I was able to forgive myself. I had so much guilt and shame from thinking I had brought it upon myself, that somehow the rape was my fault. The flashbacks, in combination with therapy, helped me to realize that wasn't true. It wasn't true at all.

It was hard, *very* hard. But I worked my butt off. I wasn't there to fiddle around. When they gave me an assignment, I did it like nobody's business. I put my all into it because God had given me hope in that jail cell, and I *knew* things were going to be different. I just had to keep pushing.

I wasn't suicidal anymore. I didn't want to evaporate. Sobriety was good.

I was tired of just surviving. I was excited about life.

I was ready to live.

I have a picture of how I looked when I went in. The emotional pain was etched all over my face. I also have a picture of me when I left. They are totally different pictures—just as I was a totally different person.

Even more, when I got released, I knew I was going back to school to get my bachelor's and master's degrees. I was going to be a therapist, come hell or high water.

I was convinced it was my calling from God.

* * *

But not everything came up roses as a result of my time at the clinic. Two weeks after returning, I was let go from my job. Apparently, the panic attack, and the assumptions about my mental state that went with it, did me in. I was never told, but I believe they made their decision while I was away getting treatment.

Talk about getting the air knocked out of me. Sometimes, life has a way of testing your commitment, and my commitment to sobriety was certainly being put to the test. I stayed on the couch for two days, and not long afterward went back to Alabama to receive some outpatient treatment to cope with that final blow. Yet I came to see that God was working, even in that injustice. The loss of employment set me up to be able to return to school that much more easily. God didn't want me to stay in sales. He wanted me to pursue becoming a therapist. God used all of that for good, and not just for my good, but for the good of others.

Along with losing my job, I experienced another negative life event—this one more far reaching and complicated. The person who handled most of my rape therapy at the clinic was a lesbian who was married to another female. She was five years younger than me, and she was a very good counselor with a master's degree. She treated me special, and I was full of gratitude toward her. Problem was, I didn't realize how special she was treating me—and, in time, she crossed the line. Others warned me about her, but I didn't listen. I liked her, too, not from a place of sexual attraction, but from an appreciation of how much she was helping me.

The woman ended up being my girlfriend, and the relationship we had was so significant to me that I ended up moving to Alabama after getting my bachelor's degree at Campbell University in August 1993 to be with her. I chose to go to graduate school at the University of West Georgia in Carrollton, Georgia, which was about a 50-minute drive from where I eventually lived with her for a time in Roanoke. I sent my longtime roommate packing, sold my home, left my parents, and moved.

The on-again, off-again toxic relationship lasted several years before it ended.

She was drawn to me when she should have been holding boundaries, and at that time, I didn't know anything about boundaries. She was a therapist. I was in desperate need of help, and I was thankful to her because I had healed so much from the work that she did with me. When she asked me to start calling her every Friday night to check in and make sure I was okay, I didn't think anything about that. I did what she told me. Then, as I realized she was sharing personal things with me that went well beyond my therapy, she'd apologize and even admit she shouldn't be doing it. But I said it was okay because it was my nature. It took being hit upside the head with a two-by-four for me to realize she was attracted to me. Someone had to come right out and tell me.

I didn't know my head from a hole in the ground, but in many ways, I was exploited by someone who had an ethical obligation to protect and facilitate healing. Ultimately, I have been able to take responsibility for my own actions that contributed to the relationship. But there's no doubt it should never have happened to begin with. Therapy is a highly vulnerable process, and I know she took advantage of that power differential.

As a therapist today, I am extremely careful to establish and maintain boundaries with my clients. I'd never want them to go through what I did—because that relationship devastated me. Anyone who comes to therapy needs to do so without anything (or anyone) competing for their attention. A relationship shouldn't even be on the radar. She is no longer practicing as a counselor. Several years ago, I told her I would report her to the licensing board if she went back into counseling for two reasons. First, having anything other than a therapist-client relationship is inappropriate, unethical, and a reason for the loss of a professional license. Second, although I cannot speak professionally about her mental health, I can state that her poor judgment exasperated some of my pain, which was contrary to the point of therapy.

Although I am thankful for the progress I initially achieved in my treatment with her, I left that relationship with more to process than I had going in. It is my sincere hope she is able to get the help and healing she needs without being exploited herself.

Chapter 5

Setbacks and Sorrow

"But he said to me, 'My grace is sufficient for you, for my power is made perfect in weakness.' Therefore I will boast all the more gladly about my weaknesses, so that Christ's power may rest on me. That is why, for Christ's sake, I delight in weaknesses, in insults, in hardships, in persecutions, in difficulties. For when I am weak, then I am strong."

2 Corinthians 12:9-10

Right after my life-altering, 30-day stay at the clinic in Alabama, I returned home to North Carolina and made plans to return to school. I went to Campbell from January to August 1993, then moved to Alabama to begin my graduate studies. I continued attending my AA meetings before and after the move, and even began speaking at AA events. Incredibly, the first time I spoke, to a group of about 100 people, I shared about the rape. My sponsor didn't think I should do it, but I truly had no fear. I had already started healing. It was an early glimpse at true freedom.

To look around and see people crying, I thought, *Okay, they can cry. I don't have to get upset with them for that.* Their tears were indicative of the pain I should have been feeling for myself. I knew I really touched some hearts that night, and that was important for me. I was so thankful I didn't follow my sponsor's guidance, and that was when I realized it was time for me to change sponsors. I had outgrown her. I even began sponsoring people myself for the first time.

The therapist gifts within me were starting to grow. I had matured and healed to the point where I was now giving back—and I loved it.

After arriving in Roanoke to live there, I started my master's studies. They were completely paid for by North Carolina Vocational Rehabilitation. That was such a God thing! During graduate school, I began working full-time as the primary therapist at a 20-bed clinic in nearby Valley, Alabama. I was operating much like a clinical director treating dual diagnosis (addiction and mental illness). All of our work was done in a group setting, and I had people who had been molested as children, physically abused, and raped, as well as many war veterans suffering from PTSD. I also worked with folks who had lost children or endured other very traumatic events in their lives.

I was in my element. That work was to die for. I loved group therapy, and given that I was functioning as director, I could basically do it the way I wanted. I used a very structured approach. My passion for what I was doing was instinctual, like breathing. I was in the trenches, doing down and dirty experiential therapy and role play, and people were being healed! In one group, a man who had been a dope dealer fell apart on the floor during therapy as he admitted that he had shot and killed a man during a drug deal. The healing that man experienced was un-freaking-believable. I equated the healing I saw in him and others with the healing I was continuing to experience myself. That's why I was so good at it. Even then, I knew that it was a gift from God. I was not fearful to take those people to the darkest abyss. I knew they could touch it and come back out without it swallowing them whole.

At one time, I'd had a murderous rage inside me. I'd discovered I could have easily killed the three men who raped me had they been placed in front of me. I would have tortured them. But I didn't like that feeling. I had to really work on it because I didn't want to have that darkness in me—and through therapy, it was eliminated.

God gifted me and healed me through the abilities He'd given me as a therapist—but I had both only as a result of going through traumas in my life and coming out the other side with His help.

I worked at the clinic for a year until it closed the following summer. From that point on, I did consultation work with several different facilities in Georgia and Alabama handling adult intensive outpatient dual diagnosis. During those engagements, I implemented a comprehensive program and pushed the envelope in showing their therapists how to use group therapy and role play to address dual diagnosis. It was awesome work.

I did all that while remaining actively involved with AA, about five hours each week, as a speaker and sponsor. I still had my own sponsor as well. I was living in Bowdon, Georgia after completing my master's degree, and I was working toward my Ed.S., which is a postgraduate specialist in education degree considered more advanced than a master's degree. I even rented a home from one of my professors. There, I tended to a retired racehorse stallion on the property, and there was a bond between me and that animal that I simply can't explain. I knew then that I loved horses and felt a strong connection to them.

I had direction and purpose. I was becoming what addiction had tried to steal from me.

Unfortunately, I had to stop pursuing the Ed.S. one semester short because I chose to move back home to Sanford.

My family life had come full circle.

Mom and dad were in failing health, and they needed my help.

* * *

I was 38 when I moved back home to Sanford in early 1996. Both of my parents were in their eighties. My dad had numerous skin cancers from playing golf and severe arthritis. Mom had osteoporosis and macular degeneration. They both had heart disease and high blood pressure. They were pretty sound in mind, but the house and yard were too much to keep up with by themselves. They had a large home on the golf course, I had the entire second floor to myself, and we decided to have some renovations done to the house. My presence brought new life into them, and being home assisted in keeping them in fairly good health while taking care of things on the property. I'm an avid yard worker, and I did some home improvements. I got the house repainted and did other things to spruce it up. They hadn't done anything like that in quite some time.

It was great to be home with my parents. I set up some boundaries and took on a leadership role in the home. At this stage of my life, I was beginning to get clarity on just how dysfunctional my family had been when I was growing up—when I felt so alone. It wouldn't be until much later that I fully realized, understood, and could heal from all of that. But I know now that the process started when I returned and took up that caregiving role with my parents. For the first time, I got a real life glimpse of the saying, "Hurting people hurt people." As I began to realize how I had been treated, it was less about me and more about them and the ways they were unhealthy, even if those ways were unbeknownst to them. I learned that unhealthy people often do not know they are unhealthy.

As I did that, I also took a job at a large residential facility, an experiential treatment program for adolescents. I was the assistant administrator there, but I was more like a clinical director. It had two campuses, one for girls in Siler City, North Carolina, and the other for boys 20 minutes away in Pittsboro, North Carolina. I had never worked with adolescents before, and I'd never thought I wanted to, but I fell in love with them. We had some really tough kids. Some were adjudicated, meaning they were under the supervision of the court. Others had conduct disorders, the predecessor for antisocial personality disorder. We had kids that had been severely traumatized and abused, and some were very volatile. Their stays with us ranged from three months to well over a year, and they learned anger management, how to deal with emotions and past traumas, and how to process their feelings so that those who were capable could be restored to their families.

I think about that now and chuckle at the irony. There I was, working to restore families after coming from such a dysfunctional background. There is no doubt in my mind today that God sent me there for a reason. Adolescents are a hard population to work with, but I absolutely loved them—probably because then I was still much of an adolescent myself.

While my work was underway at the center, a friend and contractor went to work at my parent's home renovating and completing the upstairs. He put in a bathroom and some walls—and sometimes his adopted teenage son joined him. The boy had been extremely abused as a kid. My friend and his wife had fostered and later adopted him. He wasn't too different from the adolescents I worked with at the treatment facility. The summer of 1996, a fire started upstairs where the work was being done, and the entire floor was decimated. It was so surreal how everything was fine one instant and then looked like a war zone the next. The fire was so powerful it blew out the skylights and windows, and I lost everything I had accumulated over the years since high school, including all of my sports memorabilia. The loss was estimated at over $100,000.

We'd ultimately discover that the son started the blaze. He didn't admit to it until years later, after he had been caught setting other fires. I had seen this behavior in many of the traumatized adolescents I worked with. My parents and I were thankful to have been able to get out in time without injury, but the fire was still a devastating event for my parents. It was sad and disorienting for all of us. Insurance covered the fire and the cost of mom and dad staying at a hotel. The case wouldn't be solved, though, for years. While a new contractor, a dear friend of mine, worked to rebuild everything, I stayed in the downstairs portion of the house alone for a while to make sure nothing was stolen from the rest of the home. By the time mom and dad were able to return, his work was turning out wonderfully, and we settled back in as best we could.

Back at the treatment facility, along with assessments and admitting, I chose to do a boy's and a girl's therapy group to meet licensing requirements, all while overseeing the clinical program. It was tiresome work, but it was also how I got so good at accurately diagnosing clients. I got a real feel for a kid, already formulating a diagnosis, prior to even sitting with them clinically. Most came in with some sort of a diagnosis already, which also taught me a great deal. It was a large program with as many as 150 kids being treated, and I knew every single one of them. I didn't stay in an office. I made my rounds. I was a hands-on kind of provider.

I carried on with my weekly AA responsibilities as well. I was busy, thriving as a therapist, and, for the most part, I was happy.

Then, Friday, January 24, 1997, on a freezing cold afternoon, I got a phone call at work.

It was my mother. Dad had been in a car accident.

She knew nothing more, other than that he was being taken to the hospital, and I left right away. As I drove, I thought about my mom, who just the week before had fallen in the garage and fractured her hip. She was pretty much immobile and, therefore, couldn't join me.

I was on my own. I was the strong one, so I was the one to take care of things. I always had been.

When I arrived and was allowed back into the ER to see him, dad was in bad shape. He had severe head trauma. His skull was cracked open. His left ear was gone. He had a broken clavicle. I could barely recognize him.

He was extremely lucky to be alive. I found out that he was driving on U.S. 1 when the sun got in his eyes. He did not come to a complete stop, rolled right out in front of a speeding pickup truck, and was t-boned. He wasn't used to driving an actual car. He'd been motoring around in a golf cart for so long, he'd gotten rusty behind the wheel of a real car. With mom on the mend, he'd decided to run to the little country post office. He was hooked on sweepstakes mailings, convinced he was going to win a million bucks someday, and was on his way to send in his latest entry. By all rights, he shouldn't have made the trip. But he had, and now his life was in the balance.

My father was in shock, but he was lucid enough to have a conversation—at least briefly. We talked Duke basketball. Golly, we loved the Blue Devils. Dad even had a hat autographed by Coach K. Three days earlier, Duke had whopped North Carolina State for win number 15. We were sure they were going to go all the way in March.

Not long afterward, the doctors had to intubate him, and from then on, he was no longer awake. He was placed into a medically induced coma so he could tolerate the intubation. Dad was then transferred to an emergency hospital in Chapel Hill (about 25 minutes away and, ironically, at the University of North Carolina, Duke's arch enemy on the court). He was placed in cardiac intensive care, and he stayed in CICU for the next 14 days. Dad was quite the little fighter. He died and came back three different times in that period. I remained in Chapel Hill. I spent the first several days on a couch in the waiting room. Then I ended up renting a bed, giving me my own little hospital room where I was finally able to take a shower. I never left. I was at the hospital the entire time, and I kept mom updated. My youngest nephew and niece came from Maryland to care for my mother. I truly do not know what I would have done without them. Even if she could've, mom didn't want to come, and I didn't blame her. They had been married for 63 years. She didn't want to see dad like that.

After 12 days, they finally took him out of the CICU to a different room at the hospital, he was off the ventilator, and he was talking, alert, and making sense. He was in good spirits. The plan was to get him a bed at a nursing home or a rehabilitation facility. I had promised both my mom and dad that they would never go into a nursing home. Dad talked to mom on the phone, and when he hung up, he motioned me closer to the bed.

"I want to go see my mom and my sisters," he said quietly.

They were all dead. Tears welled in my eyes.

"Why don't you do that?" I gently told my father. "I'm going take care of Dorothy, your wife, and I'm going take care of me. You go be with your mom and sisters."

I went home that evening and returned to the hospital the next day, a Friday. I visited with him like I normally had before. He shared what he did the day before, and he seemed stable. Even though I was utterly exhausted emotionally, I made a decision to go to Alabama for the weekend to see a friend and try to relax.

I'll always regret that choice. My father passed away Saturday, and I flew home Sunday morning to make arrangements for the viewing, funeral service, and cremation. He was 89.

That was a hard time for us, and I was thankful I returned so quickly and that I was there for my mom.

I was being the strong one again, but this time, it was

okay. I was able to do the things that needed to be done, take care of her, and keep her spirits up.

We muddled through.

* * *

With mom, I discovered it is true what they say about old people. If they break a hip, they never recover from it. Yet my mother had a wonderful personality and a great sense of humor. We pranked and joked with each other all the time. I called her O.B. (Old Bag). We had the best time laughing and being with each other. I cooked, and we had some really good quality time in the months following dad's death.

Then I got an opportunity in February 1998 to take a new job in Florence, Alabama, and mom and I decided to sell the house in North Carolina and have her move with me. While I went to find a new home for us in Alabama, I began working and we arranged for mom to travel to Maryland for a few weeks to see my youngest nephew, her grandson, and to visit her other grandchildren. I started my new employment and house hunted in nearby Killen.

But there was a problem with my mother, one that I didn't recognize because she was such an intelligent woman, and also because she had been in her longtime home environment and around other people that she knew—until she got to Maryland. She began getting disoriented and flustered. She forgot things such as where she was and even who she was. Then she had the first of a series of transient ischemic attacks (TIA's or mini-strokes). I'll never forget the first time I got a call and was told she was being taken to the hospital in D.C. My nephew and his friend picked me up at the airport—and they were high on dope. Here I was, an addiction specialist, and they're stoned? I was fit to be tied. I almost throat punched both of them!

I got to mother's room, and for three hours no one came to look in on her or attend to her. Meanwhile, I'm sitting there, watching her go into full-blown pneumonia. I finally went out and found a doctor. I was spitting nails. "I watched her slip into pneumonia!" I told him, a little fella who appeared to be from India. "She didn't have it the last time you saw her. I am going to put her on my back and carry her out of here if you don't do something!"

I could tell he felt bad, and thankfully, he went right to work. That doctor went above and beyond. After our tense moment, he was very good and caring to my mother. As she was going in to get an MRI (magnetic resonance imaging) exam, the same doctor and a neurologist pulled me aside and gave me the news.

Mom had Alzheimer's disease.

She was released a couple of days later and went to stay with her youngest grandson in Solomons Island, Maryland. I went straight back to Alabama to find us a home. The home in North Carolina wouldn't be sold for another year, and I ended up going back and forth with mom about once a month to keep up the yard and move some things to our brand-new house in Killen. I gave mom the master bedroom and got her a gorgeous suite of furniture. She'd never had new bedroom furniture.

I set things up for me to take care of her. I was glad to do so. Mom needed me, I was the strong one, and I always would be.

* * *

I set up an adolescent intensive outpatient program (IOP)

in Florence. An IOP is used primarily to treat such conditions as eating disorders, bipolar disorder, unipolar depression, self-harm, and chemical dependency that goes beyond a brief detoxification period. I did that for six months and absolutely loved it. I was then asked to be the clinical director of their adolescent inpatient treatment program and convert it from a 20- to a 40-bed facility. They had a mess on their hands, but I came in with expertise from my background at the adolescent residential facility and the hardened kids I dealt with there. I was quite a shock to the staff because of the experience I had with adolescents, and I knew what needed to be done. I told them I'd dedicate one year to get that program up and running, knowing it was going to demand 12- to 16-hour days. It was nothing for me to be there all night watching those kids, many of whom were gang members.

I hired a whole new staff. I implemented training and security, put in new types of furniture, and created a goal-based behavior modification program. It was a ton of work, and I made a lot of really good changes—but I did it all while living with my mom and taking care of her. Since she couldn't be by herself because of the Alzheimer's condition, I hired a sitter to be with her while I was at work each day, which was made even longer because it was a one-hour drive there and back.

All of it put incredible wear and tear on my body.

The stress I placed myself under was intense.

Too intense.

Hepatitis C can lie dormant in someone without them knowing it for years until a trigger, such as stress, draws it out in all its draining glory. When it manifests itself, sufferers can develop symptoms ranging from nausea and loss of appetite to severe fatigue. I was diagnosed with hepatitis C in December 1998, nearly a year after mom's Alzheimer's condition was made official and almost two years after my father's passing.

It had all finally caught up to me—but I didn't stop going. I couldn't. I blasted ahead as best I could while taking ribavirin and giving myself interferon shots, which are a form of chemotherapy. I had never felt that sick in my life. It was painful just to breathe. I did that all the way into and through 1999, blowing out my thyroid in the process and dealing with depression that was at times overwhelming. It was so horrible. I had passive suicidal thoughts almost every day. There was one time when I was at home talking to my boss on the phone. I was continually on call because I was training new staff and fielding room placement calls for the kids we served. I had a knack for knowing which kids would get along with each other. As I spoke with my supervisor, I felt an overwhelming sense of heaviness—like I just wasn't going to make it through another minute. In that moment, he knew how bad I was. He could hear the lack of fortitude and confidence in my voice. He could also tell I was really tired.

I was in a bad place. There was a constant, severe fatigue and no zest for life. I was losing my hair, so I shaved my head. Often, I just wanted to disappear, but I knew that wasn't an option. I didn't have a plan to kill myself. I knew I wasn't going to. I just wanted the pain to stop. I didn't want to die, but I sure didn't want to live like this. The interferon injections and blown-out thyroid caused by them magnified my depression, and I already suffered from clinical depression to boot. My meds were changed to help me. It was an extremely difficult time in my life.

At the same time, mom continued to deteriorate. She had to be placed into a hospital bed in her bedroom, and

I moved into her room and slept there so that I could
be with her more directly. She always wanted to talk
when I came home. She was excited and wanted me to
be interactive, but I'd been talking to other people all day.
In the evening, people with Alzheimer's get sundowner
syndrome, where the fading light seems to trigger wors-
ening symptoms that can continue throughout the night.
During these episodes, they are prone to get up and
wander, as well as experience increased delusions. Mom
and I usually ate dinner together in our room, watching
television and eating from little TV tables. She loved to
watch old western movies filled with cowboys and Indians.
Once she got really upset.

"Jeannie!" She was almost in a panic. "You need to let
those horses out of the corral."

"What in the world are you talking about?" I asked.

"The horses are gone!" she declared, fear in her eyes.

Then I realized what had happened. She thought we
had horses and the Indians had come and stolen them.
I chuckled inwardly, but it was so sad. The dividing line
between fantasy and reality was slowly but surely dissolv-
ing in her mind. Her episodes only added to my strain
and sheer exhaustion.

Years later, some of my coworkers told me, "You never
realized how sick you were," and they were right. I didn't.
I was too busy to realize it. As mom kept fading, I kept
working—until I parted ways with that organization
over some decisions the leadership made that I could not
abide. Before I got into the mental health field, a mentor
back in graduate school had told me, "Jeannie, I need you
to really know your values and ethics in this field because
you are going to be pushed to the limit, and you always
want to fall on the side of your values and ethics."

That's exactly what happened in this case. I could no longer fall under the line of authority because of the decisions they made that I felt negatively affected patient care and safety. I wouldn't bend, and even though I was the clinical director, when it came down to a choice between the patient and the dollar, they always chose the dollar. I could no longer be a part of that, so I left there in October 1999.

As the ridiculous Y2K fears came and went and a new century dawned without worldwide catastrophe, I kept grinding it out through my own personal upheaval. I was home with mom, making sure she was taken care of, and it was good, but taking care of her needs became more demanding than ever. She was losing herself right in front of me. To her, sometimes I was her younger sister, Willa, not her daughter. That was especially heartbreaking for me—as was seeing somebody who was once so full of life and very intelligent become a shell of a person. I began grieving for my mother as though she had already passed away. She used to hate it when I put her in the bathtub. I'd let her soak, knowing it was good for her, but she was scared of slipping. It was all so very hard.

In one of her increasingly rare lucid moments, mom said, "I never imagined the day in a million years that my baby girl would be the one taking care of me," but it was always set up that way. She might not have known that, but I certainly did. Yet I am very thankful that I was in a place where I could do that. Mom truly did not want to go to the hospital. She wanted to stay at home with me because she didn't want them to keep her. She probably felt she might not come back.

Mom didn't want me to return to work, either, and I probably could have stayed home. Mom had a rather good pension from civil service, a benefit from when my father was with the school system in D.C. But it would have been tough for me, and I knew that. So, I took a new job with a mental health center as an in-school therapist in September 2000. When I started, I said I didn't want to supervise. I didn't want to manage people. I just wanted to be a down and dirty therapist with adolescents. I was still sick, in that I hadn't completely recovered from the interferon. I also had hypothyroidism, which I didn't have prior to administering the interferon, and my immune system was compromised because of the virus. The effects of the hepatitis C lingered for years to come. I could get sick at the drop of a hat, which was made more likely being around all those kids.

Yet within three months, I was promoted to children's coordinator. Three months after that, I became program director of all their services in Lawrence County. It was everything I didn't want to do. Did the leadership, and the responsibility that came with it, happen naturally in the midst of everything by default, or was it because I couldn't help myself? It was probably a combination of both. I am a leader to a fault, and I'm a good leader. I am gifted in mental health, a gifting that came from God. I love the challenges, and even though I was trying to feel better then, I remained engaged in my work. Even then, my whole goal was to eventually go into private practice. I used to say that all the time. I should have done it, too, even with the situation with my mother, but I still didn't know then if I was good enough. Could I make it on my own? What if I failed? After all I'd overcome, that self-doubt was still there, holding me back.

*　*　*

That first Christmas of the new millennium was the strangest and saddest of my life. We had a bad snowstorm and the electricity went out on the adolescent wing. I gathered kerosene heaters and rigged them up, and I stayed there because the weather was so awful some staff couldn't get in while others couldn't get out. My mom stayed at a friend's house with her mother and grandmother. They picked her up and took her in. When I was finally able to get away to meet them on Christmas Day, we stayed there that night before mom and I were able to return home.

As 2001 started, mom was completely bedridden. She had bed sores. She had urinary tract infections that went into sepsis as her body's response to the chemicals released into her bloodstream to fight the infection went out of balance, causing damage to her internal organs. On January 17, I called for an ambulance. When the person on the line asked if my situation was life-threatening, I said "no," and they didn't come. I don't know why I said that. I guess I didn't know for sure. Either way, I had borrowed a friend's car just in case I needed to take my mother to the hospital because I couldn't fit her properly into my truck. I carried her to the car, and when she was in, I gave her a Sprite to drink, one of her favorites. She couldn't even swallow it. She was no longer there.

After arriving at the emergency room, my mother lingered for a couple more hours before she died. It was a relief when she finally passed, but I was devastated.

Looking back now, how I survived everything that happened those eight years up until mom's death was God—and sheer freaking determination. Let me tell you, that level of determination is a gift and a curse. Through it, I had accomplished a lot of things, but it was also blocking me from being dependent on God. I was so dependent on myself that I didn't see God. Even today, I have more willpower in my little finger than most people do in their whole bodies. But I don't say that happily. It has really caused me some serious problems. It has affected my relationships, in that if someone is not strong enough to handle themselves, they're not in my league. I have to have somebody in my life who I respect and who can challenge me. If they can't, I'm not interested. I can be submissive, but others have to earn and maintain my respect to deserve that submission.

Over the years, people have described me as the strongest person they'd ever met. I guess that was supposed to be a compliment, but it is a double-edged sword. If there was a challenge in front of me, I was going to take care of it because I'd always been a mover and a shaker—and I did just that, until I realized that I needed to be dependent on God. I had to be weak to let Him be strong. I had to learn to be second in command.

I'd learn that. Later on.

But at the moment, mom was gone. I was alone. I was the strong one.

Somehow, I had to stay that way.

Question was, how?

Chapter 6

Salvation and Identity

"I have been crucified with Christ and I no longer live, but Christ lives in me. The life I now live in the body, I live by faith in the Son of God, who loved me and gave Himself for me."

Galatians 2:20

"For you died, and your life is now hidden with Christ in God. When Christ, who is your life, appears, then you also will appear with him in glory."

Colossians 3:3-4

After mom passed away, all hell broke loose.
I was tired, *so* tired. I didn't want to be the strong one any longer. Frankly, I wasn't sure if I had it in me. But I had to take care of everything after mom died. I had no other choice.

I contacted my nephews and niece up north. My idea was to take mom's ashes to D.C. for a memorial service there, but it was difficult to come to an agreement on a plan. Discussions became tense. During a phone call with my niece, my mother's only granddaughter, we came to an impasse. When I hung up, I knew things had been said in anger. I also knew that mother's memorial was instead going to be in North Carolina where my mother and father had lived for the last 30 years.

I was so angry—and so weary. Now I see all of that anger was just as heavy as all of my responsibilities.

Many of my high school and work friends came to the memorial in North Carolina, and the church was packed. No family member was there, but it was a beautiful ceremony.

It would take me years to get over the loss of my mother. When I lost her, the thread that still connected me to my family was severed. When I returned to work, I was in deep grief. It changed me. For the longest time, it was kind of like I didn't do anything. I went to work. I cut grass. I went through the motions and did the minimum. A friend who knew me then described it by saying it felt like I was in a tomb. My mother was the most important relationship to me, and when I lost that, I truly *was* all alone.

In response, I worked—a lot. After becoming the county program director in March, I worked 45-50 hours a week. I oversaw all programs including a preschool day treatment service, an adult intensive day treatment program, and adult, adolescent, and children outpatient services. At different times in the years ahead, I'd also provide court liaison services, services for a community corrections program, parenting education classes, and domestic violence groups. I still lived in Killen, which was in a different county and a 45-minute commute each way. I'd always lived in a different county from where I worked because I wanted to maintain boundaries, keeping my clinical and personal life separate.

That was a good thing, because my personal life was a mess. In December 2001, nearly a year after mom's death, I was still grieving, I was unhappy—and I was extremely lonely. As a result, I met a woman online through a dating site. She was several years older than me, and I saw her on the weekends. She was an animal lover. She had horses, dogs, and geese. We also loved to cook, though we sometimes tried out different restaurants. Occasionally we went to area festivals, but we were pretty much homebodies. We watched movies and enjoyed one another's company. It seemed like we had a lot in common.

Yet I was incredibly codependent, looking for my happiness in somebody else, wanting her to make me feel better. That is codependency at its best, even with the progress I'd made with the alcoholism and in my own therapy. I was in the midst of my grief. We were both lonely, too, meaning that whatever we did together was done so that we *wouldn't* be alone, and that was no way to build a relationship.

That relationship was off and on for the next eight years before it ended—and it wasn't going to be the last.

* * *

During that time, from 2002-2010, I had no desire to do drugs or drink alcohol, but I still hit two to three AA meetings a month. I also struggled with poor stamina and a compromised immune system, the aftereffects of the hepatitis C, and my work increased. With little exception, that became my life.

By the end of 2003, I began to feel like I needed to move from Killen, eliminate my long commute to and from work, and become more a part of the overall community in Lawrence County. I put an offer on a 26.2-acre place that had a stall barn for horses, a hay barn, and a small house that had been remodeled several times. The land was the big selling point because I wanted to have horses of my own. I had already purchased my first horse in summer 2003, and I was boarding her in Lawrence County. She was huge, about 15.2 hands of muscle, a beautiful bay Quarter Horse named Big Red. It took a while, but I bought the property and moved there in June 2004. When I moved Big Red onto my property, I purchased another mare, Goldie, and I eventually bred them. The first two foals were born in April 2007.

It was the first time I worked in the same county where I lived, and Lawrence County and the town of Moulton near my ranch was an out of the way place where good ol' boy politics ruled the day. I found myself often sitting on a stool at the John Deere place picking the brains of the old men there about forage—and I loved it. I'd always been a country girl at heart, and I was definitely in the country.

The home, land, and caring for my horses lifted my spirits a bit, but the move created new stress. My place in Killen stayed on the market for another year before it sold, and paying mortgages and expenses on both places strained my finances. Meanwhile, at work, I jumped through hoops and did everything they wanted me to do, all while getting further and further away from providing direct services. I was becoming more unhappy and losing enthusiasm for the job quickly. Plus, with my money as tight as it was, I felt trapped because I was a single woman dependent on my salary. I had always wanted to go into private practice and knew I needed to do so, but I was afraid to step out and take the risk. I stayed at the mental health center because of the perceived job security it brought.

I was experiencing chronic burnout. Things were tough there—and they carried on, largely unchanged, for the next several years. By 2010, my weekend relationship was unhealthy and about to end, and that left me more vulnerable than ever. Work was wearing me out, and while I truly loved my property and my horses, they offered little solace for the turmoil that seemed to define my life. All I had been through, all I had overcome, and all I had become—and it still wasn't enough.

Then, in the summer of 2012, a couple, Julie and Chris, stopped by the ranch. They had noticed the horses and my pastures, and they wanted to know if I could board their horses. We got into an in-depth conversation about it, and as I was wheeling and dealing, they mentioned that they attended Epic Church, which was located about 13 miles down the road from my house.

They indeed boarded their horses with me, two absolutely beautiful Tennessee Walking Horses named Lady and Silver. Both were big horses. Chris also had a secondary horse named Squirt that was probably the best riding horse of them all because he was trained with kids. I loved their horses, and I liked them, too—well enough that when they asked if they could have their small group from their church meet out on the ranch property, I agreed to it. Not long after that, another couple who were dating visited and asked if I had a place for their horses. Thinking they might have heard about me from Julie and Chris, I asked the couple if they knew them.

"Sure! We go to church with them!"

More people from Epic Church? I thought. *What is going on here?*

As that was happening, work crawled along, and I hired a lady to run my day treatment program. She was having personal issues and had just recently divorced. She was about 11 years younger than me, and I could tell she respected me. She called me one evening to make me aware of some grief issues she was going through, and I provided support and encouragement as I would have for any of the staff. Then, when she called again a couple of weeks later, the conversation had a different feel—and definitely took a different turn.

She began. "If you were ever interested in going out—"

I interrupted her. "What did you just say?"

She repeated herself, and we talked a bit more before I told her, "I can't do this because of the boundaries. You work for me. I am going to have to tell my superiors. This isn't okay."

As soon as I got off the phone with her, I called my boss. "We are going to have to bring her in and talk to her and make sure everything you said is what she says," my boss told me.

"I totally get it," I replied. "That's why I am calling you."

"Are you interested in pursuing a relationship with her?" my boss asked.

There it was, and I surprised myself—a little, anyway. "Not unless I'm clear and free. I don't want any ramifications to my job."

She said they would have to move her and once she was moved, I could pursue a relationship.

In no time, the center cut her salary because it did not have a lateral move available for her. In fact, they moved her to a facility in another county. She told me she could not afford to live where she lived, and I should have said, "Tough crap!" But no. I rescued her. More than that, I allowed her to move into my home.

That was October 2012. It was a decision I would come to regret.

I was with her for about three months—and she totally hit my codependency and knocked the wind out of my sails. I didn't have family, and she had three girls who I became very close to in that short time, especially the youngest. We rode horses into the early morning hours. We had a ball. Yet it quickly became apparent there were serious problems. I ignored all the red flags, those old feelings of disgust and self-loathing resurfaced, and I totally lost all confidence in my decision making. There is no one to blame but me.

I became severely depressed before I finally broke it off, but the short-lived relationship created some real ripples at work. I was transparent about it with many of my lead staff and people under me. I wanted them to know what had happened before they heard it from somewhere else, but that only placed a target on my back. The gossip was widespread and destructive. It wasn't about her. It was about me. I felt I continually had to defend myself. Though I had followed proper channels before beginning a relationship, my integrity appeared to be on trial.

I was losing myself—again. It was worse than my mother's death, probably because I still hadn't completely dealt with her loss at that point. It was a compounded grief, but I was determined to do things differently this time. I reengaged with an old AA sponsor who was well versed in codependency. I increased my 12-step meetings, and I slowly began peeling back the layers of the codependency onion. It was big and deep, but it was the beginning of my healing.

It brought me to my knees.

Literally.

It became the catalyst that brought me to Jesus Christ.

* * *

Back in June, I started having a bonfire every Saturday night. All kinds of people came, and I was a little wary sometimes because I didn't know everyone, and it was my home. It was mainly horsey people, and folks just started showing up when word got around. I had two riding arenas that were probably a good half acre each. I had arena lights, and we rode horses into the night. People also brought out guitars and harmonicas. We had a ball.

Of course, the majority of the attendees were from Epic Church. They'd introduce themselves, and they were nice and all, but I couldn't help but think it was like a conspiracy—a conspiracy to get me into church, something I hadn't done with any regularity since my childhood Catholicism. I was still wounded from that experience. I'd never forgotten my first Holy Communion, the one where I asked the nun to explain what happened in the confessional box and she declared, "If you don't understand, then you are going to hell!"

Well, if there was a conspiracy afoot, it worked. God was establishing relationships with Christians and laying the foundation for me to go to church prior to and during that bad relationship with the woman from work. He knew I was going to need it. By the time I attended my

first service at Epic Church in March 2013, that relationship was over—and let me tell you, Epic was unlike any
church I'd ever experienced before. The inside was painted
flat black and everything was dark except for the stage,
which was bathed in spotlights. It had music and flashing
lights and smoke. People were dancing with their hands
up in the air.

It looked like freedom.

I thought "church" was going into an ornate sanctuary,
making the sign of the cross, and genuflecting (kneeling
on a bench), and here were all these people whooping and
hollering up a storm.

Oh my word! I thought. *This is like a nightclub!*

When the pastor got up to speak, I nearly passed out
when I saw he wasn't wearing any shoes. I'd never seen a
barefoot preacher before!

These people are crazy!

But any reservations I had faded away when the pastor
started speaking. He resonated with me, just like that
speaker at the AA meeting all those years earlier, but deeper.
It was more profound and even more personal. He spoke of
freedom—or, really, what I called healing, because so much
of what he talked about I had also talked about on a daily
basis as a therapist. He was transparent and genuine.

Back in the jail cell after my third DUI, I'd asked God
to help me. I had experienced a feeling, just a sense, of the
presence of the Lord and of hope. Since then, while I had
protected my sobriety and had discovered my purpose as a
therapist, I had been through so much struggle and loss. I
had started a journey with the Lord, but I had never developed the intimacy that I truly desired to have with Him.

The gift that the pastor gave me that morning at Epic
Church was the realization that I could indeed experience

complete freedom through following Jesus Christ. I had never been saved. I didn't understand that—yet. But I knew something else, something new, had been opened within me.

Shortly after that, the pastor sent me a friend request on Facebook. I didn't know this man from Adam, but I thought it was significant that he wanted to communicate with me. I messaged him back, and we set up a phone call with the associate pastor. During that conversation, I asked about their stance on homosexuality. He told me they believed it was a sin, but that they also loved people where they were and that their heart attitude for God was most important.

I visited the church a few more times that summer before I started attending regularly in the fall of 2013. That included getting involved in one of their small groups, like the one that had been meeting out at my ranch. I found out these groups were organized out of the church's Freedom Department, and the first class was called LIFE: Living In Freedom Every Day. These groups met in someone's home. The one I joined was made up of me, two other single women, and the rest were married couples.

I suppose I should've felt like a fish out of water, but I never did. I knew the group leader's wife because she worked at the veterinarian clinic where I took my animals, and we hit it off. I liked the group, and as I began praying at home, God directed me to start engaging every single person in that group. When I made the first move to reach out, it really broke the ice. It required some vulnerability on my part, something I was unaccustomed to, but somehow, I didn't feel so vulnerable with this group.

I also began to question my Catholicism and who God really was. In every group, I sat beside a woman named

Christine. She had been raised a Catholic. I asked her, "I was christened. Does this mean I am saved?" I had heard about being "saved" before, but I didn't understand it because we didn't use that term in Catholicism. She said, "I had that same question," adding that she had just gotten baptized. It was like I was a little baby. It was all so new. They were talking about things in the Bible, and I don't remember ever studying the Bible. As a Catholic, I studied missals, books containing the prayers, important chants, and necessary instructions for the celebration of the Mass. I had heard Bible stories, but we never really got into the four Gospels or the Scripture itself.

From then on, I couldn't get enough. It was exhilarating, and I had tremendous enthusiasm. I just couldn't wait to learn more and get involved. I read the Bible and went from listening to country music and classic rock to only Christian music. I worked on my cursing, I really watched what I said, and God helped me with that. I began to *change*. People noticed. It was incredible! I sensed that God was working on me. I had gone back on a couple of dating sites, but the desire to start another relationship was completely gone. That blew me away.

Then in October, during the third LIFE class, God whispered in my right ear. People laugh at me when I tell them this, but I promise, it is the truth. I always hear the whispering in my right ear, and I sometimes want to take my hand and flick Him off my shoulder because I don't want to hear what He is telling me. It had started happening after the end of the tumultuous three-month relationship with that woman from work. He'd tell me, "You are not an alcoholic. You are not a lesbian. You are a child of God." God was working on my identity as a person.

At the meeting, He told me to tell everyone what He had been telling me.

He wanted me to tell them about my past and bring it into the light.

The group leader stood up and said, "I have something fantastic to share with y'all." But I could barely hold my tongue. I was ready to bust wide open.

Before he said another word, I revealed everything just as God had directed me to do—including how I had been living a lesbian lifestyle.

We never did get to hear what he had to say. I could tell they were surprised. There were some mouths open. But they knew it was a very transparent moment, that I was being vulnerable. Everyone gathered around me in a circle and prayed for me. They prayed that I would continue to chase God, let Him work on me, and be the woman He had called me to be. I wasn't condemned. I wasn't judged. The people at Epic Church simply loved me—and their simple love was profound. It was like salve to my beat-up soul.

As I drove home that evening, I felt very much part of the group, very light and full of love. The experience confirmed what I was already beginning to realize: God *was* working on me and calling me to be the woman *He* wanted me to be—and that woman was not a lesbian woman. He began to show me that being a lesbian was not an accurate identity for me. It was one that I had chosen because of my trauma. I thought a relationship with a woman could be different than that with a man, and that I could not be hurt like I had been with men.

Hurt like I had been *by* men, the men who had raped me.

I started to see that my lesbian identity—from that earliest same sex attraction with Colleen as a child, to my first same sex relationship with my friend on the women's league volleyball team, and every relationship with a woman since—had been a deception, a masquerade, if you will. It was how I had been kept up in the bondages of my past trauma and the extreme codependency it fostered. Did I live a lesbian life? Absolutely. Did I believe that I was lesbian? Absolutely. Did I have same sex attraction? Absolutely—but my same sex attraction was very much emotional rather than physical. In my life, I had been sexually traumatized by both men and women.

I had owned that I was a lesbian—but I no longer knew if I ever *was* a lesbian.

My sexuality simply did not fit into a cozy, easy-to-unwrap box, but it was a result of confusion from years of sexual assault and violent rape. I would not fully understand it until many years later.

From that day forward, God slowly and lovingly started to show me the identity He wanted me to have—the identity that He had created me to have all along.

That was also the beginning of me starting to really trust God and walk the walk as a believer in Him. The following Sunday, the pastor spoke about turning toward Jesus and following Him if we wanted to serve God, heal our hearts, and change our lives. It was the first time I'd ever heard an altar call. I knew it was moving me. "If that is you, and you are deciding to follow Jesus," he said, "repent and make Jesus your Lord and Savior." He repeated the sinner's prayer, and I said it. He then asked us to raise our hands if we had prayed that prayer with him, and I did! I began to cry tears of joy, cleansing my soul.

Remembering what my Catholic friend had said in LIFE class, I made sure I bugged them half to death about getting baptized. I was set on G-O, and there was no backing up!

I've got it, and I want more!

God was speaking to me—and it was amazing.

* * *

Epic Church performed baptisms when there were enough people on the list to do so, and the next baptism was set for Sunday, January 26, 2014. In the meantime, I began learning about my new life as a born again Christian in LIFE class. We talked about how our relationship with God goes from justification (the event of God removing the guilt and penalty of sin) to sanctification (the process of being transformed to be more like Christ). I also attended their Friday-Saturday LIFE conference in December 2013. I remember it as if it were yesterday. During the conference, people called anointers worked with us to help us surrender and let go of things. Boy, you want to talk about powerful? I bawled like a baby. The healing, grace, and mercy of the Lord was profound.

The biggest area of healing for me regarded "soul ties," a spiritual connection between two people that comes into existence either after they have been physically intimate or following an intensely close spiritual or emotional relationship. It is where you have opened up your heart to a level of intimacy that should only be for a married partner. I had a couple of women on the emotional/sexual side, but it was nothing compared to the men. A lot of my soul ties were one-night stands, and I couldn't even list all of the soul ties I had. There were just so many. I cried from the deepest recesses of my soul while pointing to the paper where I'd written my list. The anointer who worked with me was Amanda, and as she hugged me and I tried to speak, my words were unintelligible, but it was like she knew what I was trying to say. She also knew exactly what to pray and how to break the chains the soul ties had on my life. I sobbed through the remainder of the conference as the dam broke, and I let all the deep, dark shame come out of my broken heart while letting God's light and freedom in. I was so full of gratitude and thankfulness. It's as though I could literally hear the chains hitting the floor—and, in the process, the Lord was defining my identity and who I am in Christ.

Much later, God would help me recognize and break even the soul ties made with those who had abused me.

The new year, 2014, arrived, and I began a new Freedom Department class called Victory Over the Darkness, based on a book by Neil T. Anderson. Then, the day before the baptism, my little Yorkie, Zoe, was killed. She got hit by a car right after she escaped from under the fence. My eyes were swollen shut because that was my baby, and I guess the enemy, Satan, thought that would be my Achilles Heel. I didn't let that happen. I got baptized anyway.

The baptism announcement featured a little blurb I had written, including the story of how I had met all these people from the church at my ranch. My LIFE group leader and the pastor performed the ceremony, using one of those big chemical tanks found at a tractor supply store. When I was in the water about to be immersed, the group leader said, "She says it's because of her horses she got saved." I looked at him and wanted to smack him. That was not *exactly* how I said it, but I guess it was the common thread in the way it all played out.

Then I was dunked.

As I came up out of the tank, I yelled at the top of my lungs, "Jesus!"

With that declaration, I identified with Him.

Jesus!

My identity was now fully in Jesus.

I couldn't wait to see where the new Jeannie Lynch was going to go next.

Chapter 7

Change and Crushing

"Being confident of this, that he who began a good work in you will carry it on to completion until the day of Christ Jesus ... And this is my prayer: that your love may abound more and more in knowledge and depth of insight, so that you may be able to discern what is best and may be pure and blameless for the day of Christ, filled with the fruit of righteousness that comes through Jesus Christ—to the glory and praise of God."

Philippians 1:6, 9-11

The Victory Over the Darkness class focused on who I am and Whose I am, reinforcing my identity in Christ and teaching me all about having the "mind of Christ." (1 Corinthians 2:16) Wow, were my eyes being opened! Because of my own self-condemnation, I felt so dirty about my entire past, not just the things that happened to me, but the things *I* had done to me. I learned that if I said to myself that I was dirty and bad, the enemy would use it against me. That was my weak point and his foothold.

My thoughts and my words were actually opening a dialogue with Satan that I needed to shut down. This is when I first learned that one of the enemy's greatest strategies is to make me think that his words are my thoughts. If I had known those thoughts were from the enemy, I would have been able to reject them more easily, but I didn't. As long as I bought into them, they would keep me stuck. When I read in 2 Corinthians 10:5 about the need to take my thoughts captive to make them obedient to Christ, it knocked my socks off. I am a cognitive behavioral therapist, and I have been practicing this theory of psychotherapy to help people find ways to behave by changing their thought patterns for over 30 years—yet I had no idea the science was stolen from the Bible! Taking thoughts captive and replacing them with what you know to be true is straight up Scripture. Challenging irrational thought patterns speaks to coming against what the enemy wants you to think about yourself. It was an amazing class.

Several folks from small group were asked to write a short testimony to be used for the five Easter Sunday services coming up that weekend. Church leadership requested that all of us be there on Good Friday for a team meeting. We were called on stage individually while either a man or woman read our testimony. I was the last to be called. Even though I had spoken numerous times before in front of crowds regarding the sexual assault, this was very different.

That same month, I began working part-time at the local Tractor Supply store, my first non-therapy job in quite some time. As a team lead, I oversaw other staff, and closed the store every night that I worked. I really enjoyed it because I had animals, I knew people who came in, and we'd often get to talking about horses. If that had been my only job, I surely would have excelled at it, eventually managing or even ending up owning a store of my own.

The 20 hours a week I spent there, in addition to my continued work as program director at the mental health center overseeing services in Lawrence County, was the outcome of an agreement I had made with the Lord: that a year later, in 2015, I would leave the job at the mental health center so I could go into private practice. I informed my supervisor that this was my plan for the future. I wanted to help with a smooth transition for a new program director.

It was a massive commitment inspired by my salvation and baptism experience, but it made sense. God had begun working on my identity in every other way. Why wouldn't He also go to work on my professional identity? He knew I'd wanted to go into private practice for a long time. Why not? My fear of not being good enough had kept me from stepping out. But I was learning about God and His character. I was learning about His promises, being obedient to His Word, and even about something brand new to me, spiritual warfare, in the Bondage Breaker class (another Neil T. Anderson book) that followed the completion of Victory Over the Darkness. I was learning about how God views me and the world around me. A refinement and a transformation were taking place in my heart, soul, and spirit.

Now, everything was different because *I* was beginning to change.

But it wasn't going to be easy. While things stayed on the upswing in terms of my spiritual life and growth as a Christian through the rest of 2014, I continued to work the two jobs despite increasing stress and fatigue. Then, when I had what's called an Individual Freedom Appointment (the culmination of the series of classes I had been taking at church) with a facilitator and prayer partner in February 2015, I was gently prompted to consider if I had a problem with pride.

I totally denied it. "Nope," I said, and we went on.

That would come back to get me later.

Not long after that appointment, a trio of bad things happened at the mental health center, all within a couple of months of each other. First, I was in a crisis situation with two clients, including one who had been found not guilty by reason of insanity by the courts, and the police had to be called. I was the lead authority in the situation and had two other staff members with me. In the second incident, a client was shot and killed by deputies. But it was the third event, the death of one of my staff members in a van accident during my shift, that was most devastating. I wanted to go to the funeral, but I didn't have weekends off and Tractor Supply was requiring all kinds of documentation for me to take the time away from work. I ended up resigning from Tractor Supply in June because I just couldn't keep it all together, and I felt I had to be at that funeral.

I stood beside my supervisor from the mental health center at the service—and right there, without consulting at all with God, I told her I was definitely staying at the center. It was the place that was draining me, but it was also my career. I was operating out of my fear for security and a paycheck. Before leaving Tractor Supply, I had paid off some debt. I still had my commitment to God about going into private practice. But in that moment, I allowed my fear to dictate my direction, and in my emotional exhaustion (and possibly pride), I acted on impulse.

Turned out God was not happy about that, and He let me know in short order.

I was at the center two more months before things deteriorated, and I was given a choice. In the end, that was a kindness, allowing me the option to resign. Without knowing it then, I was in chronic burnout and severe adrenal failure, manifesting as fatigue, irritability, discontent, and an overall depressed mood. I was burnt to a crisp. I wasn't enjoying my job. Fact was, I hadn't enjoyed it for years.

Even if I didn't know it yet, God knew I needed to move on and fulfill my commitment to Him, but the only way I was going to do that was if He slammed the door—and He did. He used my supervisor to move me.

I resigned August 16, 2015. Within the next week, I sent "thank you" notes to the director of human resources, the clinical director, and the human resources assistant thanking them for everything they had done and for the opportunities they'd given me. It would have been nothing for me in the past to tell them to shove off and let them feel the wrath of Jeannie, but that was not how this went. My new spiritual life was informing my behavior. It was all well with my soul. All three people are friends of mine to this day.

The following weekend, at God's direction, I went away to be alone with Him to listen and hear His will for me. I went to Joe Wheeler State Park and rented a cabin with no television, no phone, no nothing. All I took was a Bible and a journal. Even though I had known for a long time that I was going to go into private practice, my confidence had been shaken. Gently and lovingly, God showed me that I was in chronic burnout and helped me to realize the wear and tear I had been placing on my body, mind, and soul.

When I returned from that weekend, I knew without a doubt what His will was for my life.

Two weeks before the resignation, I had refinanced my house and had $12,000 that I planned to use for desperately needed renovations to the house. Instead, I used it to start my private practice—Jeannie Lynch, LPC-S, NCC, LLC—on September 16. I opened an office in Decatur, Alabama and hung my shingle.

I did what God had told me to do.

I also moved forward the way He wanted. A lot of folks advised that I should not make my practice faith-based because it would limit my clientele, but God assured me that He'd take care of me and send me the exact people I needed to see. That was a big step of faith since I did not have a caseload from the mental health center to take with me. I started from scratch. God also instructed me to use my name in the practice's brand—something I would not have chosen—because He said folks would recognize my name from years spent in the public non-profit, private for profit, as well as the recovering community. It made me a little uncomfortable, but I'd decided this was God's business and He was allowing me to run it.

That fall, as I taught a LIFE group through Epic, I started slowly with my practice, contracting with the state Department of Human Resources to supplement my caseload. At the close of 2015, I came into the office one morning to find a letter from an elderly woman whose daughter had been in a LIFE group with me. In it was $2,000. They believed so much in what I was doing, and she was insistent she didn't want me to pay it back. It was a gift. It was really hard for me to take a gift like that. I didn't receive well. Had I known it was coming, I probably would've tried to stop it. I still struggled with feeling worthy of such kindness, and I'd later learn my pride was also affecting my attitude.

*   *   *

From the time I started my practice, it took me about six months to physically start feeling like a human being again—but by early 2016, I was no longer feeling sick. That was a good thing, because it was right after the start of the year when I committed to take part in the Epic Church Leadership Institute (ECLI), an intensive 15-month leadership program that pushes class members to be the best version of themselves physically, mentally, and spiritually. This program is used to refine leaders for ministry.

I'd first heard about it and considered enrolling the year before, but God had told me then to wait. I guess He'd known what 2015 was going to be like. When the Lord gave me the go ahead, I began the application process, which included getting a medical physical and an in-person interview with the two lead pastors and three associate pastors. Before that interview, I told myself there were two things I was not going to disclose, and I was definitely not going to cry. I ended up crying and revealing both: the truth about my sexuality that I had first shared in the LIFE group, and that I didn't like feeling vulnerable because it was scary for me. It must've been okay with the pastoral team, though. I found out I was accepted for the program between Christmas 2015 and the start of the new year.

ECLI was, in a word, tough. There were academics and

theology, reading books and writing papers. We learned about everything from effective time management and spiritual warfare to relying on God in our everyday decisions and responsibilities. Oh, and then there were the demanding physical workouts while at the same time going on a strict paleo diet. To this day, I've never experienced anything quite like it.

I've also never dealt with my personal pride the way I did during ECLI. The outright denial of my pride problem back in my Individual Freedom Appointment the previous year came back to get me good. I found out just how much pride I had. Boy, it was everywhere! I was ate up with it. (That's how you say that in Alabama.) I discovered that I would *not* let people in, not be vulnerable, and was always the strong one. I wouldn't even let people bless me, all because of my doggone pride! I didn't want it to look like I *needed* anything from anyone else. At one point in the program, my fellow team members had to carry me on a makeshift stretcher as an exercise in trusting and helping one another. I'm telling you, I would have rather had a hysterectomy. It made me feel weak that somebody else had to take care of me. I had never let anybody else take care of me. It was awful—and exactly what I needed to learn.

Through ECLI, God was carefully (and, often, not so gently) pruning my pride away, and to say it was uncomfortable is an understatement. It hurt—but He was with me every step of the way, continually refining me to become the woman and leader He wanted me to be.

As much of a workout as I was getting spiritually, it wasn't much better on me physically. Being extremely ultra-competitive was in my blood, but I ended up being injured quite a bit. I had a torn rotator cuff and a stress

fracture on my right foot. The old athlete in me was used
to playing through pain, but they wouldn't let me do that.
Even that was about my pride. My ego wasn't the only
part of me getting bruised.

God also built my character through what I learned
during ECLI. When I was at the mental health center and
before, I did a lot of the right things, but I also tried to
get by with skirting some of them. When you supervise
people, you really have to be consistent across the board.
I did have favorites, but I got all types, too, and I didn't
deal with them as well as I should've. The Lord showed me
a lot about patience and tolerance that probably would
have helped me back at the center had I not been so
burned out. In the end, ECLI taught me the importance
of doing the right thing because it *is* the right thing, and
nothing else.

The Lord did a real work in me through ECLI. I grew
to know my pastors and appreciate their hearts for how
much they poured into us. Through it all, I have met some
truly incredible people who I love dearly, and to this day
would stand in the gap for them (Ezekiel 22:30). Included
among them were John and Jana Lovelace. I was immediately drawn to both of those remarkable individuals, not
knowing then that Jana was to become my best friend,
confidante, and ministry partner. I loved her personality,
and we "got" each other's sense of humor, which was really
cool. I had a super connection with her partly because we
were both therapists, but also because our strengths and
weaknesses were very similar. We were cut out of the same
cloth. She has a zeal for Jesus. She chases Jesus, and so
does John. More than very dear friends, I consider them
to be surrogate family. I had been praying for years for
people who were like-minded, high-quality individuals

that I wouldn't have to lead. He has blessed me with that in Jana and John.

It was also during ECLI that I met Keri Aycock, who became a worship leader for No Limits, and Chastidy Lynch (no relation), who is a No Limits staff member. There was also Kelly "Belly" Dutton, my laughing partner in crime. ECLI had to decorate for all the events that were happening at Epic Church, and it was nothing for us to be there some evenings until midnight or later. Kelly and I would be so tired we'd just start laughing at anything. We'd laugh so hard we cried.

God knew exactly what He was doing as He weaved this beautiful tapestry of people together. I'd later refer to this team of individuals as my tribe—which was so significant for someone who had always felt so alone.

I'll never forget, near the end of ECLI in April 2017, everyone was asked what their next step was going to be. I was surprised at what came out of my mouth.

"Well," I said, "it is time for me to share my testimony, share my life story, and there is a book, too."

*   *   *

Right after that, I decided to stop taking my anti-depressants. I had been on them since I was 32 years old. What possessed me to do such a thing? Spiritually, I had convinced myself that I wanted to try living without them. I had heard in church that God would heal my depression, and the connotation was that you are not spiritual enough if you're on anti-depressants. "Well, if you will give it to God," or "If you had the joy of the Lord, you wouldn't be depressed," or "If you would trust Him more, you wouldn't struggle in that way." I wanted to be "spiritual enough" and trust God. God can and will heal you, but again, this can happen in different ways. How the Lord heals one person may be different from the way he heals another. In addition, the way I hear someone when it comes through my filter may not be the way it is intended.

Back then, I would have told you that it was God who was directing my choice. But it was more about Jeannie. I really didn't seek God's counsel. I thought I was operating in God's will—but it was *my* will. Maybe there was some pride in my decision, too, even though my pride had already been worked on big time through ECLI.

I had to work with a doctor to be gradually weaned off the antidepressant. The one I was on will give someone brain zaps, little electrical shocks, and will resemble schizophrenia if you come off it too quickly. As I did this, I continued running my practice, and things went well until my caseload started to dry up between Thanksgiving and Christmas 2017. As my income decreased, the depression started coming back, slowly at first, but then with a vengeance. By February 2018, I had hit rock bottom without even realizing it had happened. God allowed it all, and He used it for my good, but oh, how painful it was! I was having horrible anger, irritability, and discontent. My sleep patterns were jacked up, and I couldn't get enough rest. I didn't put it all together until I talked to Jana. I told her I was having suicidal ideations, she told me I was depressed, and I honestly didn't remember what that level of depression was like until I talked to her. I realized I was experiencing what I used to feel when I was trying to get sober. I wasn't going to take a drink, but I sure did think about blowing my head off. It was a chemical imbalance in my body. Just like a diabetic needs insulin, I needed medicine.

We have to be careful, especially in the Christian church community, about what we are saying to people who may have mental illness. Ideally, pastors, or any counselors in a church setting, should be given appropriate training to discern when something is a spiritual problem they can adequately address versus when it is a mental illness that a therapist, with clinical expertise, should handle. Then those individuals should be referred to someone like me to work on their chemical imbalances in a therapy setting while the church's role is to address the spiritual side of the issue. It is all about us working together. For a person to experience true freedom from anxiety, depression, or other mental illness, they need both spiritual and clinical treatment. It is akin to a hand and a foot; they are two parts of the same body.

As my depression started resurfacing during the holidays of 2017, I became good friends with Dr. Yvette Rice. She was a co-pastor at New Genesis Community Church in Decatur, and she was also starting a new business. Yvette was a former engineer, program manager/trainer for the Department of Defense, and a government contractor for the United States Army Corps of Engineers. She was one sharp, spiritual woman. When she asked me to do a women's workshop with her at a church in town, I kept feeling like God didn't want me to do it. Yet she told me that she saw me speaking and that women from all over were going to come. She said I was going to be telling them my testimony.

I thought she was crazy.

As my caseload started to dwindle away, God began to tell me to get my ducks in a row and prepare. I didn't know what I was preparing for, but I did what He said and started to prepare as if I was going to have an influx of clients. Jana and John came in and did business planning with me, and Jana even ended up creating a website for my business. Every now and then, Yvette would ask, "How are you doing?" I'd say, "God told me to prepare."

Other than what I had to pay my bills, I had no money. After I went into a debt relief program, I had to have a colonoscopy that ended up costing me about $12,000. Several of those medical bills went into debt relief. I didn't want to file for bankruptcy. I just buckled down and kept moving forward.

To this day, I refer to this time in my life as the "Crushing." The term came from the title of an incredible book by T.D. Jakes, and my crushing was the severe depression that came from being off my medication combined with my financial crisis. In his book, Jakes wrote that "Crushing," the time when God turns pressure into power, required dying to self—all of that carnal humanness that holds us back from being who God wants us to be. It was painful. I have always been independent. I thought I could do it all on my own, but that wasn't true. I couldn't do it all myself, and that certainly was not what God wanted. The Lord had to hit me in every area of my life—personal, social, financial, spiritual, and physical—*crushing* me so that I had to surrender and fully become dependent on Him.

It almost broke me. It was hard as H-E-double-toothpicks.

But in it all, God was there.

He allowed it all for my good—and through it all, breakthrough was about to come.

I just had to *not* quit five minutes before the miracle happened!

Chapter 8

Happy Endings and Beyond

"But we have this treasure in jars of clay to show that this all-surpassing power is from God and not from us. We are hard pressed on every side, but not crushed; perplexed, but not in despair; persecuted, but not abandoned; struck down, but not destroyed. We always carry around in our body the death of Jesus, so that the life of Jesus may also be revealed in our body."

2 Corinthians 4:7-10

My crushing went on for about four months—until the second week in March 2018 when I had an influx of 20 clients *in one week.* That is absolutely unheard of. I got people from church. I got people from referrals and from the mental health center where I used to work. The phone was ringing off the hook. It was just booming. There is no doubt in my mind God broke the dam.

That was why He had been telling me to prepare. He was waiting for my obedience.

I had been speaking to Yvette daily about God, faith, and what He was doing in our lives, and that became a real constant for me. I trusted God, and I knew He was going to stay true to His promises in the Bible. He had called me to have my own therapy practice, and I realized that my crushing had been a time of preparation so I could carry the mantle of being His therapist. It didn't let up, either. I started getting up to five new clients a week, and my schedule began filling up. I had to develop a virtual office and hire a client coordinator to take all of my calls. I already had a person to oversee insurance and billing so I could focus on seeing clients.

After much prayer, I went back on antidepressants, and I gradually started feeling better. I found that I was able to hear God again; not that I couldn't hear Him before, but it was harder when I was depressed and not feeling good. Another important result of being back on medication was that I gained a deeper appreciation of, and empathy for, my clients, and of the struggles we dealt with together: clinical depression, anxiety, addiction, bipolar disorders, and so on. I understood anew that so many people coming into Christian churches have mental illness or mental health issues that are serious: partly spiritual, but partly clinical. I could pretty much tell when a client needed to be on medicine and when they needed to do some spiritual work, but in some cases, they couldn't address the spiritual matters unless they first had the medicine. Medicine clears the fog, so to speak, allowing a person to think and see clearly. It realigns the brain chemistry so that folks can function on a level playing field.

God has created and given wisdom and knowledge to those who make antidepressants and those who prescribe them. It is another way toward healing. There is no shame in my game about taking meds. They are part of what God used to heal me.

While all of that was going on, I was also leading a women's small group study at Epic Church in the Freedom Department. We were studying Bondage Breaker, the last of the three-part series. Fourteen women participated, and in November 2018, we rented a cabin that was more like a chateau on a small lake in scenic Rising Fawn, Georgia. The cabin only slept eight, but we squeezed in, got cozy, and made it work for 14 people. It was one of the best weekends I've ever had. We had women from 18- to 78-years-old from all walks of life—a school principal, a teacher, a massage therapist, a homemaker, a physical therapist tech, a retiree—and everyone shared testimonies about what God was doing in their lives. We did an exercise where they looked into a mirror, read a letter they had written to someone in the group they emulated, and watched as we discovered they were actually reading about themselves. It was so encouraging and restorative. We even went ziplining. Everything was fun, and we had a such a good time. We were crowded as all get out in that little chateau, but that was exactly the way it was supposed to be. We really bonded on a new level.

Another completely unexpected surprise came from that weekend by the lake. Before we went ziplining, two of the ladies were sharing their testimonies, and you could hear a pin drop. All the ladies were crying, but in the middle of the second story, my phone rang. I didn't recognize the number and hit decline, but it rang again. Sometimes when I'm away, I'll get notifications about clients in crisis, so I felt I needed to take it. I answered the call. I learned I was speaking with Donna Sparks, an author, speaker, and evangelist. I'd never met Donna before, but the woman who rented us the cabin had told me Donna had stayed there the previous weekend working on her latest book. She had suggested Donna contact me.

I politely asked her if I could call her back, and then returned for the rest of the testimony. When I told everyone who I had just spoken to on the phone, they just about fell out! Many of the ladies were familiar with her books. So, I got Donna back on the phone, put her on speaker, and Donna then told us her story. It was eerily similar to the testimony of the woman who had just finished giving hers. Donna then spoke an eloquent prayer over all of us, and I concluded the call by saying, "I'll be in touch with you because you are going to speak for me. Really, not for me, but for God!"

I had no idea where that came from or what it even meant. Well, sort of.

The following Sunday, I had a Bible study in my office for some of the ladies who had graduated with me from ECLI. One of them, of course, was Jana Lovelace. When I told them Donna's testimony and what had happened in the call with her, I looked at Jana.

"Are you ready?" I asked.

"Yep," she said without hesitation.

I then looked at Keri Aycock (who would become the worship leader and a speaker) and asked her if she was ready.

"Yes," she replied adamantly.

No explanation or additional information was needed. God had been preparing us individually, so we all knew what He was communicating to us.

In that moment, No Limits Women's Conferences, LLC was born.

I called Donna two days later, and we talked for two hours. I shared some of my testimony and then told her that we were planning a women's retreat, that God was downloading information to us, and that He was leading me toward having her speak at the event.

"Absolutely!" Donna proclaimed.

Things quickly started falling into place from there. Jana and I met on Mondays and some weekends, and we did a lot of planning for the inaugural No Limits conference. Once we concluded we needed another main speaker, in addition to Donna, I went to Yvette. I told her what we needed, and she instantly replied, "Amanda Goodson." I'd never heard of her before, either, but it turned out Dr. Amanda H. Goodson is a dynamic speaker, coach, and author who also happened to be the first African American woman to ever hold the position of Director of Safety and Mission Assurance at the National Aeronautics and Space Administration (NASA).

Wow! Again, I had no idea. But God did—and He was putting it all together. We quickly realized that No Limits was not our women's retreat, but His. We were simply being the hands and feet at His direction.

In the end, we had no less than 11 incredible speakers at the event October 16-18, 2019. Donna and Amanda were the lead speakers with Dawn Mason anchoring on Sunday, and everyone was incredible! We ended up having it at Shocco Springs Baptist Conference Center in Talladega, Alabama. God had told me He wanted it in a place with leaves that looked like mountains, and that was the place. We even got to incorporate leaves as a powerful illustration. Fall colored cloth leaves were given to each of the attendees. After the break, all of the ladies (we had 120 in attendance) wrote something on the leaves they wanted to be released from, something they wanted to "leaf" behind (pun intended)! They then attached them to a large tree that was constructed in the lobby and left them there as a symbolic gesture of giving their bondages over to God. It was powerful!

I will never, ever forget that first conference. It was a long time coming, and the closeness we experienced with all the attendees that weekend was nothing like anything I had experienced in the other conferences and retreats I'd attended. All the meals were on campus. All the speakers and staff members for No Limits stayed in the bunkhouse, while everyone else was housed in the living quarters that were much like a college dormitory. We had a good mixture of races, cultures, ages, and even denominations, which was very important to us and to God. We had a large time, and the responses we received afterward were profound. There was no negative feedback at all, and one woman after another shared how No Limits had affected and impacted their lives in its mission to bridge the gap between life's struggles and spirituality. I probably got 20 clients from those attendees. That wasn't the purpose, of course, but the relationships were made. Dr. Goodson told me that she had been to conferences and retreats all over the world, and she had never seen anything like it. It was truly life changing—for those attending, speaking, volunteering, staff, and for Jana and myself.

*   *   *

The year 2019 was a whirlwind of being obedient to God. Because of my obedience, His favor flourished. The following month, November, I began writing this book. I had already contributed a chapter featuring my story to *Women in Leadership: Living Beyond Challenges*, an anthology compiled by Amanda and Yvette and published in September, as well as written another chapter for the book, *The Purpose and Power of Mentorship*. For me to be involved in three books, one of them my own, fulfilled a passion God put deep inside of me. There were even times when Jana said, "Don't you think you need to take a break?" I'd respond, "Let me talk to God first," and He would tell me to keep pressing in—and so I did, but only by His strength.

The mentorship book was published by Dr. Goodson the summer of 2020. By then, of course, the nation, and the rest of the world, were in the early grips of the COVID-19 pandemic. I had a fully functioning office where I saw clients in person, but I was already laying the foundation for a platform to meet with people virtually through a telehealth service. I was resistant to it at first because I'm an old school therapist who likes to be right in front of my clients. I prefer face-to-face interaction—but the pandemic put telehealth into play and sped up this process. At God's direction, I ended up closing my physical office, and most of my clients transferred with me to telehealth. I got a whole new computer system set up in my home with business internet and all of the requirements needed for security and privacy. I also used a lady's office in the same building in Decatur where my office was previously located to see clients I must work with in person, like couples or adolescents who are difficult to treat via telehealth, on the first and third Wednesdays of each month.

The pandemic did force Jana and I to put No Limits 2020 on hold, but as soon as the COVID-19 situation allowed, we were ready to hit the ground running. We couldn't wait to see what God was going to do through it in the years to come. In addition, I launched a new ministry in 2021 called A Servant's Heart with Jeannie Lynch which will focus on the content shared in this book, the teaching material delivered in the next chapter, and on speaking opportunities and retreat events. I believe God will use it in a mighty way to bring His healing and freedom to people's lives, especially women.

When 2020 began, before the pandemic hit, the Lord gave me three words for the year: focus, connection, and relationships. My focus was to be on God. My connectedness was to be with God and people: to listen, and then to nurture those relationships. It was amazing. I only wanted one word, but He sent me three. He knows I'm a bit of an overachiever. They were directly from Him, and they've each played themselves out in such a remarkable way.

As I've focused on God, He's told me not to worry. Everything will be in His time. I've kept my connections and continued working on them despite the challenges presented by the pandemic. I've seriously nurtured my relationships, especially with those closest to me. In many ways, while not physically with others, I have been more connected to them because it is all about being intentional in relationships. I have discovered that I can be intentional without having to be physically present.

Through it all, I have indeed learned that it's all about Him. God has healed me, continues to do so, and can heal any one of us. My healing didn't come in one fell swoop. I've learned that healing or freedom comes in layers, just like the hurt did. I'm still on my journey of healing and always will be. Just when I think I am fully healed in one area, God takes me to a new level of healing that I did not know possible in another. He is such a good, good Father. The Lord does love broken people, and as He comes into our lives and heals us from the inside out, He will use our stories to further His Kingdom to help bring others to freedom. That is the true beauty of Jesus. He loves me the same now as He did when I was broken, but His desire for me is healing and freedom.

As I look to the future, I am thankful, empowered, and I can't wait to see what He has in store for me—and for you—next.

Chapter 9

Your Path to Healing

"He sent out his word and healed them; he rescued them from the grave."

Psalm 107:20

"Then you will know the truth, and the truth will set you free."

John 8:32

"Sanctify them by the truth; your word is truth."

John 17:7

s I wrote this book, there were some valleys as a lot of things from my past came full circle into my present. In the process, God revealed an even deeper healing that I had not experienced previously. It was very cathartic—as long as I kept my focus on

Him. In the moments where my focus shifted off of Him, it became overwhelming, but then He would remind me of my healing as I looked back to Him.

I also developed a teaching to communicate and apply to the book's title, "Don't Quit Five Minutes Before the Miracle Happens," that I will use to create a ministry toolkit for people through A Servant's Heart with Jeannie Lynch. As a therapist, I know many things makes sense on paper or on a cognitive level. But applying them to your life is a different story. My hope is that this teaching will bridge that gap. For each teaching point (1-16), there is a personal reflection meant to provide content for the teaching, and a personal application meant to help you apply that specific teaching to your life. As the Lord unfolded this teaching to me, I was again amazed, energized, and excited for me and for you!

Prepare to experience His healing touch for your past traumas as I now share that teaching with you.

* * *

TEACHING POINT #1. BE OPEN TO LEARN ABOUT GOD!

Deep down, I always knew I was missing something. Past traumas, addictions, mental illness, and a negative foundational mindset were absolutely destroying me from the inside out. This mindset included not trusting others, not showing any vulnerability, a default response of anger and rage to keep people at a distance so that I wouldn't be hurt again, remaining a victim with no boundaries, and always looking outside of myself to fill the big, black hole and void inside of me. I was so broken, and I knew it.

Psalm 147:3 declares that God "heals the broken-hearted and binds up their wounds." Through Alcoholics Anonymous, I started to learn about God. Part of learning who He was meant discovering who He was not: a punishing hellfire and brimstone God. I had a flawed view of God, and I had to undo that before I could be able to trust Him. That was really hard for me—so hard, in fact, that I almost missed Him. I made the process difficult and complex. It did not have to be, I assure you, but again, I truly did not trust Him at first. I was really hardheaded. Being raised in an orthodox religion that was based on good works really skewed me, and my stubbornness came at least in part from the abuse I suffered as a child and into my early adulthood.

Yet as I began to trust the AA group as a whole, that also opened the door for me to trust God. He knew exactly what I needed and began to soften my heart, just as Ezekiel 36:26 says when the Lord told the prophet, "I will give you a new heart and put a new spirit in you; I will remove from you your heart of stone and give you a heart of flesh." As my journey toward an intimate relationship with God progressed, I realized the truth of Deuteronomy 4:29, that if "you seek the Lord your God, you will find him if you seek him with all your heart and with all your soul." Yes, it took years because of the damage done by myself and others. But I knew something was happening—and it felt good. Unfamiliar but good. Vulnerable but good. Trusting the AA group, I began to see God and His goodness. That was a brand-new experience for me, and one I wanted more of.

Joel 2:13 proclaims, "Rend your heart and not your garments. Return to the Lord your God, for he is gracious and compassionate, slow to anger and abounding in love, and he relents from sending calamity." Once I deepened my trust in God and started seeing His true nature and characteristics, it was salve to my soul, but my curiosity had been piqued. I was hungry to learn more.

Two Bible passages supported my desire to trust God with my past traumas. One was Proverbs 3:5-6, which says, "Trust in the Lord with all your heart and lean not on your own understanding; in all your ways submit to him, and he will make your paths straight." The other was Isaiah 61:3, which talks of the year of the Lord's favor as being a time to "provide for those who grieve in Zion—to bestow on them a crown of beauty instead of ashes, the oil of joy instead of mourning, and a garment of praise instead of a spirit of despair. They will be called oaks of righteousness, a planting of the Lord for the display of his splendor." During the first two years of my recovery, my negative foundational mindset started to shift, transitioning into a place of hope. I hadn't had hope for years, dating back well before my rape. But gaining hope is what having a relationship with God is all about. To be honest, having hope was scary at times, too. It was new and different, but I knew I wanted it. No, I *needed* it.

As part of this process, I created two boxes. One was a "Came to Believe" Box. The other was a "God Box" that I will talk about in Teaching Point #2. The "Came to Believe" Box was a little index file with cards that had "God things" on them. I wrote down just enough on each one to know the past God thing and the date. It was my little box of miracles that I could open and read whenever doubt slipped in—and guess what? It worked! Good things happened, and I began to get very excited about my future. One of the God things I wrote down was when the North Carolina Vocational Rehab program paid for me to finish my undergraduate studies. Another one was how I, among the three percent of diagnosed individuals who took the specific medications I was prescribed for hepatitis C, responded very well to those medications. I didn't know it at that time, but God had totally healed me of hepatitis C. A third reminded me of how I was able to use the money from the refinancing of my home to start my private practice. To date, there are over 100 God things in my "Came to Believe" Box.

For many years, through the loss of my parents, new jobs, geographical moves, and a myriad of health challenges and relationship issues, I knew God and He knew me, but there was an aching in my soul. Whenever I felt that pain, my default emotion was anger. I also tried to fill the void with external things such as caring for horses and relationships, but I was not fulfilled and couldn't find genuine peace. I now know that peace is not an emotion. Peace is a person, and His name is Jesus.

It's only through learning about God by seeking Him and applying His Word that you can discover authentic peace for your life. I encourage you to read the entire book of 2 Samuel 22. In it, David delivers a song of praise to the Lord after his deliverance by God from his enemies. In verses 31-33, David declared, "As for God, his way is perfect: The Lord's word is flawless; he shields all who take refuge in him. For who is God besides the Lord? And who is the Rock except our God? It is God who arms me with strength and keeps my way secure." David had learned the value of God's instruction and direction during times of incredible stress and trauma when he often cried out to God, pleading to him with raw emotion to help him. You'll read these moments of pure, genuine emotion from David throughout the Psalms. No emotion (anger, doubt, disillusionment) was off the table for David—and the Lord lovingly and patiently listened, responded, and delivered his servant. The same is true for us today as we struggle.

Personal reflection

1. Name a negative foundational mindset that is absolutely destroying you from the inside out? What made it harmful to you?
2. How have you found the truth from Psalm 147:3 to be true in your life?
3. List three things you would place in your "Came to Believe" Box.
4. How can you apply these responses to make sure you don't quit five minutes before the miracle happens?

Personal application

You will experience God's deliverance and peace-giving presence as you 1) are open to learn about God, 2) willing to share your authentic feelings with Him, and 3) obey His directions for your life.

* * *

TEACHING POINT #2. I CAN'T, HE CAN, SO LET HIM.

This was a totally new concept for me. I had always been a mover and a shaker, dependent on no one. Trust me, this did not die easily. I was a very independent, strong woman who did things out of her own ability and sheer willpower. However, Romans 9:16 tells us, "It does not, therefore, depend on human desire or effort, but on God's mercy." As I started to learn how to turn things over to

God, I made my "God Box" out of a Christmas cookie tin. I cut an opening in the top and put pieces of paper inside that had things written on them like "anger and rage," "self-loathing," "cravings for drugs or alcohol," "dishonesty," or the names of difficult people in my life. The brief statements indicated more detailed things that I needed to trust God, in His mercy, to take care of for me. I held a murderous rage for the men who raped me, so I put that into the God Box so that I could position myself to forgive them. Revenge is taking poison, hoping that it kills the other person. I sometimes loathed myself, so I put that into the God Box so that I could forgive myself. Forgiveness allowed me to cut the ties to the past.

After placing things in the God Box, if I took one of those statements back *from* God and tried to handle it on my own, I'd write it down again and put it in. It helped me, as it does a lot of people, to visualize that process and live it out in a physical act. As it went into the God Box, I was letting it go. It created a sense of responsibility and accountability, and it continued the process of softening my heart in order to forgive and accept forgiveness. Unforgiveness actually ties us to the person with whom we are angry or hurt, therefore not allowing us to distance ourselves from them when that is actually what we most desire. Did you know that? But I choose forgiveness because of God's direction, even when I don't want to give forgiveness or ask for it, and especially when it hurts. It keeps me humble when the Holy Spirit convicts me, and I obey Him. Sometimes I obey instantly; other times, not so quickly, but God continues to help me to be willing to be forgiven and to forgive those who have wounded me. Sometimes I'll only wish the worst for them—but God! He softens my heart to where I can not only pray to forgive them, but I can also speak the same type of prayers I'd ask for myself. I'd pray for their families, for them to turn toward Jesus, and for God to heal them as He is healing me. Over time, I was able to forgive the three men who raped me—truly forgive them—and cut the ties that bound me to them. I did it, not so much for them, but for myself. As God has forgiven my sin, I need to forgive others (Luke 6:37). The freedom this brings is incredible!

Now, mind you, when I first created my God Box, I was not yet a Christian and would not be for many years, but the process of salvation had begun. It was slow—but oh so worth it. As 2 Samuel 23:5 says, "If my house were not right with God, surely he would not have made with me an ever-lasting covenant, arranged and secured in every part; surely he would not bring to fruition my salvation and grant me my every desire." I must say, living out this principle of "I can't, He can, so let Him" was emotionally painful at times. But I have learned that the other side of emotional pain is spiritual growth. It took time, and it will be different for every person. This is not about comparing ourselves to other people and their journeys. I had to learn to avoid comparisons. Comparing myself to others kept me stuck for a long time. But as I trusted God, I was able to move forward.

The Bible speaks of the pitfalls of comparison in the incredible story of Joseph (Genesis 37-50). Again, I encourage you to read all 14 chapters to experience the full, rich drama of the tale, but in Genesis 37:2-3, we learn that "Joseph, a young man of seventeen, was tending the flocks with his brothers, the sons of Bilhah and the sons of Zilpah, his father's wives, and he brought their father a bad report about them. Now Israel loved Joseph more than any of his other sons, because he had been born to him in his old age; and he made an ornate robe for him. When his brothers saw that their father loved him more than any of them, they hated him and could not speak a kind word to him." It gradually got worse from there, with the brothers plotting to kill Joseph before selling him into slavery in Egypt and making up a story for their father that Joseph had been killed by a ferocious animal. Throughout the rest of this amazing story of trial, triumph, and redemption, Joseph discovers time and again, "I can't, He can, so let Him."

Personal reflection

1. What things keep you from being dependent on God?
2. What would you put in your "God Box" that you cannot manage, but He can?
3. When you compare yourself to others, what does this do to you? Is it helpful or hurtful?
4. How can you apply these responses to make sure you don't quit five minutes before the miracle happens?

Personal application

Remember, your life is a journey. You'll travel it successfully by 1) focusing on the present and its gifts instead of on the destination, 2) striving to be the best version of you and who God wants you to be, and 3) always being a student and a seeker.

* * *

TEACHING POINT #3. QUIET TIME AND PRAYER.

Next, I started reading at least two chapters from the Bible every morning, and then I spent time meditating on what I had just read. That meditation included talking with God out loud, having a conversation with Him just like I would with a close friend, and then listening to Him. Since Psalm 104:34 exhorts, "May my meditation be pleasing to him, as I rejoice in the Lord," I also listened to Christian praise and worship music. Some of my favorite artists still include Lauren Daigle, Francesca Battistelli, and Hillsong Worship. I supplemented this activity with books such as Joel Osteen's *I Declare: 31 Promises to Speak Over Your Life.*

When I had attempted to read the Bible before this time in my life, my comprehension of God's Word was just not there. So, I prayed for the Holy Spirit to give me understanding of Scripture, and guess what? He did! Through His Word, my heart began to change. My anger would dissipate. I got excited to read the Bible and know God better through it. As I meditated, my thoughts ran rampant at first, but I learned to better control my thoughts. I discovered that even though the Bible had been written well over 3,300 years ago, it easily applies to my everyday life. I began to memorize Scripture so I could replace any negative thoughts with its truths. This took time and practice. Dying to self and becoming more Christ-like always does. I encourage you to find a study Bible that breaks down the Word for you by providing cross references to research and meanings for some of the Hebrew wording from the Old Testament and Greek wording in the New Testament. I use the Life Application Study Bible.

Next, I started writing down my prayers so I could actually read them to myself. Through this process, prayers that were self-centered began to change. I started praying for others. I made a prayer list and would pray for every name on that list: friends, people who had crossed my path, and people I did not know. God began nudging me to reach out to specific people through text with a prayer that God led me to send to them. Then, I prayed to God, asking Him to help me stay sober and sharing the requests that I had written down as I read the Bible. At that time, about nine months into my sobriety, it was the longest I had been sober since I'd first started drinking. I knew that was huge!

As I mentioned earlier, at first, these prayer requests were primarily about me. Selfishness dies hard, and God was beginning to work on me, but boy, did He have His job cut out for Him. He was up for the challenge. I was slowly discovering the truth of Philippians 2:3, where Paul teaches, "Do nothing out of selfish ambition or vain conceit. Rather, in humility value others above yourselves." As my prayer life developed, the Lord was just scratching the surface with the things in my life that needed to be brought forth and healed. He revealed what He needed to reveal, and He gave me what I could handle when I could handle it. A lot of people say, "God won't give you more than you can handle." No. God won't give you more than what you can handle *with Him*. Sometimes, that means He will give you precisely more than you can handle so you will look to Him. It is not in your own strength, but it is with Him, through His strength, that healing comes.

As you press in to the Lord through your quiet time and prayer, you'll discover that you are worth the commitment, the work, and the pain required to get to the other side. Asking God for help isn't easy. There were times I would have rather had every tooth in my head pulled out than to show a sign of vulnerability, even to Him. I had been emotionally hurt by people (even those who loved me the most) at such a deep level, it made me internalize the thought that something was wrong with me—that I was unlovable. I truly believed that, and I operated on that foundational belief system for most of my life. That was the greatest lie the enemy has thrown at me, and it hit me where I was the most vulnerable. The enemy's tactics have not changed since the temptation of Christ Himself (Matthew 4). The deception that I was so broken that I would never be able to overcome kept me stuck in the proverbial abyss of being absolutely miserable and totally alone, unable to have deep relationships or intimacy. That also prevented me from having a deep, intimate relationship with God. Later, I would pray for God to show me things that were not pleasing to Him and to help me, through His strength and provision, to be obedient to be who He wanted me to be.

But I have learned at my very core that *I am worth it*—and you are, too! When God presents trials in our lives, He uses them for our good and frequently causes discomfort or pain to the point where we are willing to step out of our comfort zone, grow, and rely on Him as our help. Just like Peter when he stepped out of the boat in faith (Matthew 14:22-33), we must be willing to step out for Jesus, move toward God's Kingdom purposes for our lives, and step in to being the person the Lord has created us to be. Let your faith rest on God's power, not your wisdom (1 Corinthians 2:5).

Don't quit on God or yourself. The miracle is coming! I've learned this to be true over and over in my life. You have no idea how much potential you possess through Jesus. We will often quit when we experience pain even though we actually have another 10 percent of push within us. This is actually God's strength. I see folks all around me who will put in a max of 90 percent, start to feel the emotional pain or hear the enemy's temptation to quit, and stop. We still have to press in! After all, Scripture tells us that we already come from a place of victory! How? Because of what Jesus Christ did for us on the cross.

Finally, remember that Jesus never quit. He spent time with His Father daily, going away by Himself into the hills to pray and hear from Him. He constantly sought to be close to His Father. Do the same with your Heavenly Father, and you will experience your breakthrough.

Personal reflection

1. What can you change to give God the best of you, not your leftovers?
2. What incredible lesson have you learned as you make reading God's Word your heart's desire?
3. What has happened to you as you've allowed prayer to flow from your heart to God's throne?
4. How can you apply these responses to make sure you don't quit five minutes before the miracle happens?

Personal application

As you continue to prioritize quiet time and prayer, 1) meditate on the Scripture you have read and begin to apply it to your daily life, 2) ask God to change your heart, and 3) always talk with God as you would a confidante or best friend.

* * *

TEACHING POINT #4. FELLOWSHIP.

God's directive for us is to fellowship with like-minded individuals, "having the same love, being in one spirit and of one mind." (Philippians 2:2) I attended church every

Sunday prior to the COVID-19 gathering restrictions, and I watched online services at home as the pandemic continued. I have a family of choice in my Epic Church community, and they are *amazing!* They have beautifully personified Peter's desire for us to "be like-minded, be sympathetic, love one another, be compassionate and humble." (1 Peter 3:8) I feel the same about them as Paul did about his faith family in 2 Thessalonians 1:3, where he wrote, "We ought always to thank God for you, brothers and sisters, and rightly so, because your faith is growing more and more, and the love all of you have for one another is increasing."

For someone who had not had a full family relationship in well over 20 years, finding and attending Epic Church was, and still is, a balm to my lonely heart. I am able to ask for and receive help when needed. That is a *big* one for me! It wasn't until I landed at a church where I felt welcomed for who I was that I began going deeper with God and learning more about His character and His love. That culminated with the day I accepted Jesus Christ as my Lord and Savior—and it started the journey of a lifetime! The void began to fill up with God, and I can tell you, it felt so good! I found what I had been searching for my entire life!

Accepting Jesus as my Savior and developing a deeper relationship with Him did not mean that things were going to get easier in my life. No! As a matter of fact, it became harder in a lot of ways. In Matthew 7:13-14, Jesus said, "Wide is the gate and broad is the road that leads to destruction, and many enter through it. But small is the gate and narrow the road that leads to life, and only a few find it." I discovered Christ's words to be true as I fought to deny my carnal self and become more Christlike and Kingdom minded. It was not easy, but the big difference was that I was not doing it alone, but with God. It was not in my strength, but His. It was a hard lesson to learn, but it was needed in order for me to totally surrender to Him. It didn't have to happen all at once. I am still on this journey today. God has been such a good Father. He knew I did not trust others or myself easily, and therefore, I'd struggle to trust Him. He knew I didn't receive well (from Him or others), and I had never asked for help. Yet I learned that blocking others from blessing me was nothing more than my own pride, and it was prohibiting me from having the deep and intimate relationship with God or others that I truly desired. It took the crucible of the "Crushing" for me to learn that I could trust the Lord and be dependent on Him.

Do I trust Him perfectly today? Absolutely not. But when I let go and allow Him to do His work in me, it is incredible! I mess up a lot. I will never be perfect in this world. Yet I remain on the potter's wheel (read Jeremiah 18) where I am being constantly refined as the Lord shapes me into who He wants me to be for Him and for my good. This is the sanctification process of being made holy only through the merits and justification of Jesus Christ through the work of the Holy Spirit. Sanctification cannot be obtained by any works-based process, but only through the works and power of the divine. I will be in this process as long as I am on this earth.

It is fellowship with like-minded individuals that sets the stage for such intimate fellowship with Jesus Himself and the process of sanctification that fellowship with the Lord brings. In John 15, Christ taught His disciples about the vine and the branches. Pay close attention to the illustrations He used as He spoke.

"I am the true vine, and my Father is the gardener.

He cuts off every branch in me that bears no fruit, while every branch that does bear fruit he prunes so that it will be even more fruitful. You are already clean because of the word I have spoken to you. Remain in me, as I also remain in you. No branch can bear fruit by itself; it must remain in the vine. Neither can you bear fruit unless you remain in me. I am the vine; you are the branches. If you remain in me and I in you, you will bear much fruit; apart from me you can do nothing. If you do not remain in me, you are like a branch that is thrown away and withers; such branches are picked up, thrown into the fire and burned. If you remain in me and my words remain in you, ask whatever you wish, and it will be done for you. This is to my Father's glory, that you bear much fruit, showing yourselves to be my disciples." (John 15:1-8)

Isn't it remarkable? The quality of our fellowship with Christ determines the quantity of our "fruit" in the lives of others. If we want to make a genuine, lasting difference with those around us, we must "remain" in Him.

But Jesus wasn't done revealing the benefits of fellowship. Christ said, "As the Father has loved me, so have I loved you. Now remain in my love. If you keep my commands, you will remain in my love, just as I have kept my Father's commands and remain in his love. I have told you this so that my joy may be in you and that your joy may be complete. My command is this: Love each other as I have loved you. Greater love has no one than this: to lay down one's life for one's friends. You are my friends if you do what I command. I no longer call you servants, because a servant does not know his master's business. Instead, I have called you friends, for everything that I learned from my Father I have made known to you. You did not choose me, but I chose you and appointed you so that you might go and bear fruit—fruit that will last—and so that whatever you ask in my name the Father will give you. This is my command: Love each other." (John 15:9-17)

Love. Joy. Sacrifice. All three are developed and fulfilled through our fellowship with the Lord and with each other.

Personal reflection

1. How have you benefitted from your faith family? How are you with accepting blessings from others?
2. How are you trying to be the friend that you want in your life to others?
3. How has having a group of like-minded individuals impacted the depth of your faith and the process of sanctification in your life?
4. How can you apply these responses to make sure you don't quit five minutes before the miracle happens?

Personal application

As you fellowship, watch what God does for you as the Lord 1) provides meaningful relationships through your brothers and sisters, 2) deepens your relationship with Him as you daily "remain" in Christ, and 3) increases your impact in the lives of others as you display His love and joy.

*   *   *

TEACHING POINT #5. PRAISE AND WORSHIP.

The Lord is a jealous God (Exodus 20:5) who wants His children to worship Him and Him alone—and an essential component of this kind of singular, focused worship of God is sacrifice.

It might surprise you to know that the first place "worship" is mentioned in the Bible is in Genesis 22 and the story of Abraham and Isaac. In it, God tested Abraham through what many still view as an unexpected and even shocking method. "God said, 'Take your son, your only son, whom you love—Isaac—and go to the region of Moriah. Sacrifice him there as a burnt offering on a mountain I will show you.' Early the next morning Abraham got up and loaded his donkey. He took with him two of his servants and his son Isaac. When he had cut enough wood for the burnt offering, he set out for the place God had told him about. On the third day Abraham looked up and saw the place in the distance. He said to his servants, 'Stay here with the donkey while I and the boy go over there. We will worship and then we will come back to you.'" (Genesis 22:2-5)

Notice how Abraham clearly associates worship with the incredible sacrifice he has been asked to offer. I don't know about you, but I don't think I would've been in a mood to worship knowing I was about to sacrifice my own son. What a reflection this was of Abraham's righteousness—and his righteous obedience to God—even when it was clearly at odds with his own will, and even when his heart was breaking. The story continues in verses 6-8, "Abraham took the wood for the burnt offering and placed it on his son Isaac, and he himself carried the fire and the knife. As the two of them went on together, Isaac spoke up and said to his father Abraham, 'Father?' 'Yes, my son?' Abraham replied. 'The fire and wood are here,' Isaac said, 'but where is the lamb for the burnt offering?' Abraham answered, 'God himself will provide the lamb for the burnt offering, my son.' And the two of them went on together."

I don't believe this was deception on Abraham's part. I'm convinced he truly believed God would provide the sacrifice, even if that "lamb" ended up being his child. The scene dramatically concludes, "When they reached the place God had told him about, Abraham built an altar there and arranged the wood on it. He bound his son Isaac and laid him on the altar, on top of the wood. Then he reached out his hand and took the knife to slay his son. But the angel of the Lord called out to him from heaven, 'Abraham! Abraham!' 'Here I am,' he replied. 'Do not lay a hand on the boy,' he said. 'Do not do anything to him. Now I know that you fear God, because you have not withheld from me your son, your only son.' Abraham looked up and there in a thicket he saw a ram caught by its horns. He went over and took the ram and sacrificed it as a burnt offering instead of his son. So Abraham called that place The Lord Will Provide. And to this day it is said, 'On the mountain of the Lord it will be provided.' The angel of the Lord called to Abraham from heaven a second time and said, 'I swear by myself, declares the Lord, that because you have done this and have not withheld your son, your only son, I will surely bless you and make your descendants as numerous as the stars in the sky and as the sand on the seashore. Your descendants will take possession of the cities of their enemies, and through your offspring all nations on earth will be blessed, because you have obeyed me.'" (Genesis 22:9-18)

To sacrificially give up what we love the most and offer it to God is the greatest form of worship—and such worship is a reflection of our praise, our willingness to let go, and our trust that He will provide what He knows is best for us. God rewards obedience with the *best* reward of knowing that our actions have honored our Father.

Personal reflection

1. Name two things you can let go of sacrificially as an act of worship to God. Before you answer, take a moment to pray to make sure what you sacrifice is directed by Him alone.
2. For each one of those two things, how can you praise Him in the midst of letting go of them?
3. How has praise and worship changed your mindset about your life?
4. How can you apply these responses to make sure you don't quit five minutes before the miracle happens?

Personal application

As you praise and worship, give God the glory as He 1) provides for you, just as He did for Abraham and Isaac, 2) increases your intimacy with Him as you lift Him up, and 3) continues to help you think differently about your daily challenges and blessings.

* * *

TEACHING POINT #6. SPIRITUAL WARFARE.

I began to learn about the enemy, Satan, and his attacks. Jesus identified the devil as a thief that "comes only to steal and kill and destroy; I have come that they may have life, and have it to the full." (John 10:10) In 1 Peter 5:8, we are told to "be alert and of sober mind. Your enemy the devil prowls around like a roaring lion looking for someone to devour." How does he try to consume us? Through our minds. Nothing happens without a thought coming first. In the book of Genesis, Eve had a thought about the forbidden fruit before she took a bite. Satan is the father of all lies (John 8:44) and the great deceiver (Genesis 3:13). I never realized that my negative thoughts and self-talk were actually the enemy coming at me with self-condemnation. I was 50-something years old, raised in church, and *never* knew this! It was life changing! Satan, who knows our most vulnerable and weakest parts, supplants my thoughts with his thoughts, and his tactics have not changed since his fall from heaven (Luke 10:18).

In spiritual warfare, the battleground is not flesh and bone (Ephesians 6:12), but the mind. In the past, I always believed self-condemning thoughts were mine alone, but they were not. So, I began to replace the attack of the enemy's thoughts with the truth of Scripture. What a huge difference this made! It wasn't easy. The enemy had been speaking negativity to me for so long, it felt normal. These are what we call "habitual thoughts." They are not accurate, but habitual. The more I replaced the enemy's thoughts with God's thoughts from the Bible, the easier it got. Declare who you *are* in Christ: a creation of God who belongs to Him (Malachi 2:15), a forgiven servant of the King who has been given the mind of Christ (1 Corinthians 2:16), and so on. No longer give the enemy focus or attention, for "if anyone is in Christ, the new creation has come: The old has gone, the new is here!" (2 Corinthians 5:17)

I love the Holy Spirit. He convicts me of the things I need to give over to God, and there is a big difference between the *conviction* that comes from the Holy Spirit and *condemnation* that comes from the enemy, Satan. Conviction is the Spirit's gentle nudging to repent, and the Spirit is such a gentleman. Whether He convicts me softly or not so softly, He knows exactly what I need when I need it. He does not force me to do anything, particularly if I am being hard-headed. Condemnation, on the other hand, tends to be harsh and judgmental, often in a self-deprecating way. The enemy tells me, "You will never get it right. You screwed it up again," whereas the Holy Spirit tells me, "My child, let's try that again. I love you." Whoa! That's a major difference!

One of the most notable examples of spiritual warfare in the Bible is found in Matthew 4 where Satan goes to battle against Christ Himself. Scripture says Jesus was led by the Holy Spirit into the wilderness "to be tempted by the devil. After fasting forty days and forty nights, he was hungry. The tempter came to him and said, 'If you are the Son of God, tell these stones to become bread.' Jesus answered, 'It is written: "Man shall not live on bread alone, but on every word that comes from the mouth of God."' Then the devil took him to the holy city and had him stand on the highest point of the temple. 'If you are the Son of God,' he said, 'throw yourself down. For it is written: "He will command his angels concerning you, and they will lift you up in their hands, so that you will not strike your foot against a stone."' Jesus answered him, 'It is also written: "Do not put the Lord your God to the test."' Again, the devil took him to a very high mountain and showed him all the kingdoms of the world and their splendor. 'All this I will give you,' he said, 'if you will bow down and worship me.' Jesus said to him, 'Away from me, Satan! For it is written: "Worship the Lord your God, and serve him only."' Then the devil left him, and angels came and attended him." (Matthew 4:1-11)

Jesus responded to all three of Satan's offers by quoting God's Word before commanding Satan to leave—giving us the simple and powerful blueprint to battling the devil whenever spiritual warfare directly invades our lives. We must always place Jesus' words first in our lives. The truth of the Word drives out the enemy.

Personal reflection

1. What are your most vulnerable issues that the enemy uses against you?
2. How can you become more aware of how your thoughts impact your feelings and then your behavior?
3. In what ways can you replace your negative thoughts and self-talk with Scripture? What are the differences in your thought life of conviction versus condemnation?
4. How can you apply these responses to make sure you don't quit five minutes before the miracle happens?

Personal application

When thinking of Satan and spiritual warfare, remember that 1) the purpose of the thief is to steal, kill, and destroy, 2) the devil will use anything to be successful against you, even God (like he did in Genesis 3:5 when he told Eve she would be like God if she ate the forbidden fruit), and 3) God may allow Satan to come against us if He knows it will refine us, but we always stand in a place of victory because of Jesus and His work on the cross. Fight the battle and don't quit—for when you quit, you will no longer be a threat to Satan, and you will not push God's Kingdom forward. Thus, the enemy will have won.

To aid your battle against Satan, make these biblical declarations your own.[1]

I am accepted...

John 1:12—I am God's child.
John 15:1—As a disciple, I am a friend of Jesus Christ.
Romans 5:1—I have been justified.
1 Corinthians 6:17—I am united with the Lord, and I am one with Him in spirit.

1 Corinthians 6:19-20—I have been bought with a price, and I belong to God.

1 Corinthians 12:2—I am a member of Christ's body.

Ephesians 1:3-8—I have been chosen by God and adopted as His child.

Colossians 1:13-14—I have been redeemed and forgiven of all my sins.

Colossians 2:9-10—I am complete in Christ.

Hebrews 4:14-16—I have direct access to the throne of grace through Jesus Christ.

I am secure...

Romans 8:1-2—I am free from condemnation.

Romans 8:28—I am assured that God works for my good in all circumstances.

Romans 8:31-39—I am free from any condemnation brought against me, and I cannot be separated from the love of God.

2 Corinthians 1:21-22—I have been established, anointed, and sealed by God.

Colossians 3:1-4—I am hidden with Christ in God.

Philippians 1:6—I am confident that God will complete the good work He started in me.

Philippians 3:20—I am a citizen of heaven.

2 Timothy 1:7—I have not been given a spirit of fear but of power, love and a sound mind.

1 John 5:18—I am born of God and the evil one cannot touch me.

I am significant...

John 15:5—I am a branch of Jesus Christ, the true vine, and a channel of His life.

John 15:16—I have been chosen and appointed to bear fruit.

1 Corinthians 3:16—I am God's temple.

2 Corinthians 5:17-21—I am a minister of reconciliation for God.

Ephesians 2:6—I am seated with Jesus Christ in the heavenly realm.

Ephesians 2:10—I am God's workmanship.

Ephesians 3:12—I may approach God with freedom and confidence.

Philippians 4:13—I can do all things through Christ, who strengthens me.

Let me add this. We need to recognize that habitual thinking, or our old programming in addition to how I *feel*, may not be accurate. There is a difference in *feeling* versus *fact*.

What is the truth?[2]

Our old programming / how I feel says, "I am unloved," but our blessings in Christ / what is true about me says, "I am very loved." (John 15:9, Romans 8:35-39, Ephesians 2:4-6, 1 John 3:16, 1 John 4:10 and 19).

Our old programming / how I feel says, "I am unacceptable," but our blessings in Christ / what is true about me says, "I am accepted." (John 15:15-16, Ephesians 1:3-6).

Our old programming / how I feel says, "I am unworthy," but our blessings in Christ / what is true about me says, "I am worthy." (Romans 8:31-34, 1 Corinthians 6:19-20, 2 Corinthians 5:21).

Our old programming / how I feel says, "I am inadequate," but our blessings in Christ / what is true about me says, "I am adequate." (2 Corinthians 2:14, 2 Corinthians 3:5-6, 2 Corinthians 12:9, Philippians 4:13).

Our old programming / how I feel says, "I am a failure," but our blessings in Christ / what is true about me says, "I am victorious." (Romans 8:37, 2 Corinthians 2:14, 1 John 5:4).

Our old programming / how I feel says, "I am fearful," but our blessings in Christ / what is true about me says, "I am free from fear." (Psalm 4:8, Psalm 27:1, Psalm 32:7, 2 Timothy 1:7, 1 John 4:18).

Our old programming / how I feel says, "I am anxious," but our blessings in Christ / what is true about me says, "I am content." (Psalm 4:8, Psalm 37:5, Psalm 55:22, Philippians 4:6-7 and 11, Hebrews 13:5, 1 Peter 5:7).

Our old programming / how I feel says, "I am weak," but our blessings in Christ / what is true about me says, "I am strong in Christ." (Acts 1:8, 2 Corinthians 12:9-10, Ephesians 1:19, Ephesians 3:16, Philippians 4:13).

Our old programming / how I feel says, "I am not very smart or good enough," but our blessings in Christ / what is true about me says, "I have God's wisdom." (John 15:15, John 16:13-14, 1 Corinthians 1:30, James 1:5, 1 John 2:20-21 and 27).

Our old programming / how I feel says, "I am in bondage," but our blessings in Christ / what is true about me says, "I am free." (John 8:32 and 36, 2 Corinthians 3:17, Galatians 5:1 and 13a).

Our old programming / how I feel says, "I am unwanted and belong to no one," but our blessings in Christ / what is true about me says, "I have been adopted by God and am His child." (Romans 8:16-17, Galatians 4:5-7, 1 John 3:2).

Our old programming / how I feel says, "I feel guilty," but our blessings in Christ / what is true about me says,

"I am totally forgiven." (Ephesians 1:7, Ephesians 2:13, Colossians 1:14).

Our old programming / how I feel says, "I am depressed," but our blessings in Christ / what is true about me says, "I have the joy of the Lord." (John 15:11, John 17:13, Romans 15:13, 1 John 1:4).

Our old programming / how I feel says, "There is nothing special about me," but our blessings in Christ / what is true about me says, "I have been chosen, set apart by God." (John 15:16, 1 Corinthians 1:30, 1 Corinthians 6:11, 1 Peter 2:9).

Our old programming / how I feel says, "I am hopeless," but our blessings in Christ / what is true about me says, "I have all the hope I need." (Romans 8:20-25, Romans 15:4 and 13, Colossians 1:26-27, 1 Peter 1:3).

Our old programming / how I feel says, "I feel condemned," but our blessings in Christ / what is true about me says, "I am blameless." (John 3:18, John 5:24, Romans 8:1).

Our old programming / how I feel says, "I am alone," but our blessings in Christ / what is true about me says, "I am never alone." (Romans 8:38-39, Hebrews 13:5).

Our old programming / how I feel says, "I can't reach God," but our blessings in Christ / what is true about me says, "I have access to God." (Ephesians 2:18, Hebrews 4:14-16, 1 Peter 2:5 and 9, 1 John 5:14-15).

Our old programming / how I feel says, "I am afraid of Satan," but our blessings in Christ / what is true about me says, "I have authority over Satan." (Colossians 1:13, 1 John 4:4, Revelation 12:7-11).

Our old programming / how I feel says, "I have no confidence," but our blessings in Christ / what is true about me says, "I have all the confidence I need." (Proverbs

3:26, Proverbs 14:26, Proverbs 28:1, Ephesians 3:12, Philippians 1:6, Hebrews 10:19, 1 John 5:14).

*   *   *

TEACHING POINT #7. SERVICE.

Ephesians 6:7-8 exhorts, "Serve wholeheartedly, as if you were serving the Lord, not people, because you know that the Lord will reward each one for whatever good they do, whether they are slave or free." Service is so important, and my process of learning service started with AA and continues today. I signed up for clean-up duty. I scrubbed toilets, vacuumed, washed dishes, and wiped down the AA clubhouse. I began to hang with like-minded folks. One of the hardest transitions for me was losing my so-called friends. There were so many folks that I thought were friends but, in reality, were just using or drinking buddies. We were helping to keep each other stuck. Misery loves company, you know. There was a period of approximately three to four months when I truly did not have any friends. I felt awkward developing close relationships without drugs or alcohol. I had never done that before. Eventually, I did start to develop relationships and having get-togethers that were fun, clean, and sober. This was a gift from God. I began chairing meetings and sponsoring other women newcomers to AA. I loved all of it—and God was starting to introduce me to my calling and my passion.

Years later, after being saved, service took on a whole new meaning. I had such a heart shift. I was encouraged at church to get plugged into serving. I signed up for a team based on my giftings and talents. I helped folks get plugged in to service. I prayed for individuals who came requesting prayer. I assisted people in any way that I could, and if I could not help them, I got them to the people who could. This was when I began to lead small groups, which I absolutely loved. Small groups had made such an impact on me, and I knew in leading, God was at work in my life. I began to mentor women. Rich relationships were developed as God used His gift that He had placed in my heart so very long ago to be the hands and feet of Jesus. His anointing was huge, and I loved that God trusted me enough to lead people to Him. I was overcome with joy and humility. God then called me to serve Him even further by cofounding No Limits Women's Conferences. He moved me way out of my comfort zone in service to Him. As the Bible teaches us, "Offer hospitality to one another without grumbling. Each of you should use whatever gift you have received to serve others, as faithful stewards of God's grace in its various forms."

Our ultimate model for service, of course, is Jesus Himself. John 13 describes an incredible moment that occurred just before the Passover festival—and Christ's death on the cross. It says, "Jesus knew that the hour had come for him to leave this world and go to the Father. Having loved his own who were in the world, he loved them to the end. The evening meal was in progress, and the devil had already prompted Judas, the son of Simon Iscariot, to betray Jesus. Jesus knew that the Father had put all things under his power, and that he had come from God and was returning to God; so he got up from the meal, took off his outer clothing, and wrapped a towel around his waist. After that, he poured water into a basin and began to wash his disciples' feet, drying them with the towel that was wrapped around him." (John 13:1-5)

Can you imagine how confused the disciples must've

been by His actions? Simon Peter certainly was. He asked, "'Lord, are you going to wash my feet?' Jesus replied, 'You do not realize now what I am doing, but later you will understand.' 'No,' said Peter, 'you shall never wash my feet.' Jesus answered, 'Unless I wash you, you have no part with me.' 'Then, Lord,' Simon Peter replied, 'not just my feet but my hands and my head as well!' Jesus answered, 'Those who have had a bath need only to wash their feet; their whole body is clean. And you are clean, though not every one of you.' For he knew who was going to betray him, and that was why he said not every one was clean." (John 13:6-11) I am reminded that Jesus knew Judas was going to betray him, but Judas still ate anyway.

The amazing scene concludes, "When he had finished washing their feet, he put on his clothes and returned to his place. 'Do you understand what I have done for you?' he asked them. 'You call me "Teacher" and "Lord," and rightly so, for that is what I am. Now that I, your Lord and Teacher, have washed your feet, you also should wash one another's feet. I have set you an example that you should do as I have done for you. Very truly I tell you, no servant is greater than his master, nor is a messenger greater than the one who sent him. Now that you know these things, you will be blessed if you do them." (John 13:12-17)

Personal reflection

1. What are your talents? These are directly from God. What are you good at? It can be anything.

2. What is your personal ministry? Whatever your answer, do it as if you were serving the Lord directly. In other words, do it the very best you can. Perform with excellence—and let me gently remind you, this does not mean perfection. Lean into His

direction, finding the balance of excellence versus perfection. Ask God to help you identify this and free you from it.
3. What is possibly blocking you from serving?
4. How can you apply these responses to make sure you don't quit five minutes before the miracle happens?

Personal application

God has called each one of us to serve, so 1) have a servant heart like Jesus, 2) identify your gifts and talents and begin to serve the Lord, and 3) you will experience an incredible heart shift in serving.

* * *

TEACHING POINT #8. GENEROSITY.

Colossians 1:10 exhorts us to "live a life worthy of the Lord and please him in every way: bearing fruit in every good work, growing in the knowledge of God." I became generous with my time and resources. I gave of my time to those who were suffering. If I had something that someone needed more than me, I gave it to them. I got out of myself and helped someone else. The passage from 2 Corinthians 9:6, "Remember this: Whoever sows sparingly will also reap sparingly, and whoever sows generously will also reap generously," became a principle I lived by—and in the process, God worked on my selfishness, and it really felt good. My self-esteem increased.

I also began to tithe in obedience to Malachi 3:10, which says, "'Bring the whole tithe into the storehouse, that there may be food in my house. Test me in this,' says the Lord Almighty, 'and see if I will not throw open the floodgates of heaven and pour out so much blessing that there will not be room enough to store it.'" I had absolutely no understanding of this at first, but I discovered tithing was a heart issue, and God was again working on my heart. Even though I was generous with my time, I was not so generous with my money. But the way I now think about it is this: it is God's money, and I am called to be a good steward of His money. So, that's what I do in obedience to His directives, not as an empty fulfillment of His commands, but because I want to please Him.

Every week, I take the top 10 percent of all my income and tithe to my church, as we are instructed to do in Deuteronomy 14:22, which says, "Be sure to set aside a tenth of all that your fields produce each year." I do not reveal this to boast, but to honor what the Lord has told me to do. He is making my heart generous and servant minded. I love it!

Because of my obedience (not because of the tithe itself), God has poured His favor and blessings upon me just as Colossians 1:10 promised. Do I do it for His favor and blessings? No. The desire of my heart is to please God. The favor and blessings are just a by-product. It is about obedience, not blessings. The focus had to shift from getting to giving, and as it did, it opened up my life to a whole new level of freedom in Christ! God worked on me, in His perfect timing and for His desired ongoing outcome, and He is in no way finished with me yet. There is so much more to work on. I desire to always have a soft heart to His leading and direction. I will never be done on this earth, and you know what? I am cool with that! I always want to be a student of the Holy Spirit.

Personal reflection

1. How are you serving God with your talents and resources?
2. Where is your heart right now when it comes to generosity?

3. Outside of church, how do you seek opportunities to be a blessing through your generosity?

4. How can you apply these responses to make sure you don't quit five minutes before the miracle happens?

Personal application

As you strive to live a life worthy of the Lord and please Him in every way through your generosity, 1) continually check your heart, 2) instead of only giving what is easy, give where it hurts a little while being a good steward of His resources He has blessed you to manage, and 3) always be aware of your opportunities to be the hands and feet of Jesus.

*   *   *

TEACHING POINT #9. THANKFULNESS.

In 1 Thessalonians 5:18, Paul teaches us to "give thanks in all circumstances; for this is God's will for you in Christ Jesus." I began doing just that. I was thankful for my developing relationship with God. Thankful for my relationships and my parents. Thankful for my sobriety. Thankful for my traumas. Thankful for all the things God was working out in me. The principle of Ephesians 5:20, "Always giving thanks to God the Father for everything, in the name of our Lord Jesus Christ," started changing my attitude about life. I discovered that it was impossible to be thankful and angry at the same time. The two cannot occupy the same space.

Just how thankful am I? I am humbled and eternally grateful for God's grace and mercy. I truly believe the Lord came after me. All it took was for me to take a turn toward

Him—and that was the *very* best decision I ever made. God saved me from a life of sin and destruction. It is true what is said about sin leading to chronic sin. For me, I became desensitized in following my carnal desires. Sin led to more sin. I was absolutely miserable. The enemy fooled me—yes, *fooled* me into thinking I was having fun and that "everybody did it." This was deception at its best. I did choose sin, and I had free will in all of my choices. I was in a spiritual desert. I distinctly remember the day I wept with the pure emotion of love and joy at the amazing wonder that the God of the entire universe, the great "I am," had forgiven all of my sins, past, present and future, and was making me whole. Today, I continue to be "rooted and built up in him, strengthened in the faith as you were taught, and overflowing with thankfulness." (Colossians 2:7)

The writer of Psalm 107 gives thanks to the Lord by citing the many stories of "the redeemed." It's a fabulous book of Scripture, and one that you can use to allow the Bible to be your springboard to thankfulness. The account from Psalm 107 that resonates with me the most begins in verse 23. "Some went out on the sea in ships; they were merchants on the mighty waters. They saw the works of the Lord, his wonderful deeds in the deep. For he spoke and stirred up a tempest that lifted high the waves. They mounted up to the heavens and went down to the depths; in their peril their courage melted away. They reeled and staggered like drunkards; they were at their wits' end. Then they cried out to the Lord in their trouble, and he brought them out of their distress. He stilled the storm to a whisper; the waves of the sea were hushed. They were glad when it grew calm, and he guided them to their desired haven." (Psalm 107:23-30)

That was me! But, praise God, I am now one of His redeemed—and I shall always be thankful to Him!

Personal reflection

1. How does thankfulness impact your life? Explain.
2. In what ways do you express your thankfulness?
3. List at least three things that you are thankful for right now. Start a habit of keeping a thankful or grateful journal and writing in it every day.
4. How can you apply these responses to make sure you don't quit five minutes before the miracle happens?

Personal application

Always give thanks to God the Father in the name of Jesus by remembering that 1) God loved you first, 2) His grace and mercy are yours in abundance, and 3) your thankfulness will bring about a heart change.

*　*　*

TEACHING POINT #10. BRINGING SHAME TO LIGHT.

One of my absolute favorite stories from the Bible is in John 4. There, we see Jesus venturing into Samaria, a place where most Jews of His day did not dare to tread. The Samaritans were despised, and prejudice toward them ran deep. Jesus, however, did not possess such hatred or discrimination. As He arrived in the town of Sychar, He came to a plot of ground Jacob had given to his son Joseph called "Jacob's well," and it was there He sat, tired from His journey. The story carries on.

"When a Samaritan woman came to draw water, Jesus said to her, 'Will you give me a drink?' (His disciples had gone into the town to buy food.) The Samaritan woman said to him, 'You are a Jew and I am a Samaritan woman.

How can you ask me for a drink?' (For Jews do not associate with Samaritans.) Jesus answered her, 'If you knew the gift of God and who it is that asks you for a drink, you would have asked him and he would have given you living water.' 'Sir,' the woman said, 'you have nothing to draw with and the well is deep. Where can you get this living water? Are you greater than our father Jacob, who gave us the well and drank from it himself, as did also his sons and his livestock?' Jesus answered, 'Everyone who drinks this water will be thirsty again, but whoever drinks the water I give them will never thirst. Indeed, the water I give them will become in them a spring of water welling up to eternal life.'" (John 4:7-14)

Jesus engaged the woman in conversation and started to reveal who He was to her—but He wasn't done yet. In response, the woman said, "'Sir, give me this water so that I won't get thirsty and have to keep coming here to draw water.' He told her, 'Go, call your husband and come back.' 'I have no husband,' she replied. Jesus said to her, 'You are right when you say you have no husband. The fact is, you have had five husbands, and the man you now have is not your husband. What you have just said is quite true.' 'Sir,' the woman said, 'I can see that you are a prophet. Our ancestors worshiped on this mountain, but you Jews claim that the place where we must worship is in Jerusalem.' 'Woman,' Jesus replied, 'believe me, a time is coming when you will worship the Father neither on this mountain nor in Jerusalem. You Samaritans worship what you do not know; we worship what we do know, for salvation is from the Jews. Yet a time is coming and has now come when the true worshipers will worship the Father in the Spirit and in truth, for they are the kind of worshipers the Father seeks. God is spirit, and his worshipers must worship in the Spirit and in truth.'"

"The woman said, 'I know that Messiah' (called Christ) 'is coming. When he comes, he will explain everything to us.' Then Jesus declared, 'I, the one speaking to you—I am he.'" (John 4:15-26)

The moment Jesus declared His identity as Messiah, I can hear the woman's heart. *You know who I am. You should find me repulsive and an outcast. After all, I came to the well at the hottest time of the day, when no one else was here, because of my shame. Yet here you are, the Messiah, and you reveal yourself to me?*

Instantly, the Samaritan woman became the first missionary—going to her friends in town, telling them, "Come, see a man who told me everything I ever did. Could this be the Messiah?" (John 4:29) Imagine the ground around the well hardened and cracked. The water cannot be soaked up until the ground is exposed. Yet, as the woman's heart was exposed, her shame was brought to light—and Jesus accepted her, just as she was.

My own shame, and the fear it birthed, propelled me through life. I was afraid of everything. On the outside, I was a Billy Bad Butt, but I sure didn't feel that way on the inside. I was being dishonest. I was a chameleon. Depending on who I was with, I would become like them to fit in, but I was not okay with myself. I was like the one spoken of in Job 10:15: "If I am guilty—woe to me! Even if I am innocent, I cannot lift my head, for I am full of shame and drowned in my affliction." Yet as I revealed my shame, beginning all the way back with my AA sponsor and onward since then, my Messiah has accepted me. I now drink of His living water every day and experience the truth of Isaiah 61:7. "Instead of your shame you will receive a double portion, and instead of disgrace you will rejoice in your inheritance. And so you will inherit a double portion in your land, and everlasting joy will be yours."

Personal reflection

1. What shame are you holding on to?
2. List at least two ways in which that shame affects you.
3. If you have experienced bringing light to the darkness in your life, explain how this made you feel? Shame is from the enemy. Be intentional here about reminding yourself of the distinction between conviction versus condemnation.
4. How can you apply these responses to make sure you don't quit five minutes before the miracle happens?

Personal application

As you exchange your shame for His light, always remember that 1) NO ONE is too far gone, 2) God loves you unconditionally, and 3) God knows everything about you—and accepts you fully.

* * *

TEACHING POINT #11. STEPPING OUT IN FAITH.

My journey has taught me that I can totally trust God. Time and again, He has directed me to step out of my comfort zone, have faith in Him, and leap. Yes, leap!

In late 2020, I decided to do something that had always been on my bucket list: skydive. I'd always had a very real fear of heights, but after becoming a believer in God, I desired to offset my fears with faith. So, I tandem jumped with an instructor, meaning I was strapped tightly to his front as we leaped together. The sensation when I was airborne with him was out of this world. Freeing, fun, and not scary at all—and that remained the case for me even as our parachute lines got tangled on the way down. The instructor shook us violently as he worked to free the lines so the chutes would open, but I never felt afraid, even when I knew that we were in trouble. That's not me; that's never been me. But I had peace, God's peace that is beyond human understanding (Philippians 4:7) because even if that chute hadn't opened, I knew I was still going to be okay, even if I died. It wasn't like I was intentionally thinking that at the moment, but that was how I felt. That's God!

Matthew 14 tells of such a leap for one of the disciples, Peter. After speaking to a crowd, Jesus instructed his disciples to sail out onto the lake while He went up to the mountainside to pray. Later, the boat holding the disciples was unable to return to Him because it was being buffeted by a powerful storm. "Shortly before dawn Jesus went out to them, walking on the lake. When the disciples saw him walking on the lake, they were terrified. 'It's a ghost,' they said, and cried out in fear. But Jesus immediately said to them: 'Take courage! It is I. Don't be afraid.' 'Lord, if it's you,' Peter replied, 'tell me to come to you on the water.' 'Come,' he said. Then Peter got down out of the boat, walked on the water and came toward Jesus. But when he saw the wind, he was afraid and, beginning to sink, cried out, 'Lord, save me!' Immediately Jesus reached out his hand and caught him. 'You of little faith,' he said, 'why did you doubt?' And when they climbed into the boat, the wind died down. Then those who were in the boat worshiped him, saying, 'Truly you are the Son of God.'" (Matthew 14:25-33) While Peter's eyes were fixed on Jesus, he was fine. I mean, he was walking on water for Pete's sake (pun intended)! But when he began to take his eyes off Jesus and focus on his circumstances (the wind), he began to sink.

Like Peter, I have leaped, and Jesus has sustained me as I traversed some stormy seas of my own. Out of it all, the Lord called me to start a private practice, to transition to telehealth as my main service, and to cofound No Limit's Women's Conferences, LLC. He has called me to be part of two other books and author this one. Wow! All were significant leaps of faith for me, and each one has brought tremendous challenges and blessings. I just had to keep my eyes focused on Him.

Trust me, none of this is about me. It is all about God and bringing *all* glory to Him. Now, whenever I have to make a decision, big or small, I always seek God's will—always! Have I heard a booming voice or seen a burning bush? I have not. But I *hear* God in my heart, and I know, I just know, that it's Him. I hear Him through Scripture. I have had dreams. I have heard Him through others. I have heard a small, inviting voice. God has given me spiritual antennas, and I strive to keep them constantly pointed at Him.

I was certainly glad my antennas were pointed His way back in the spring of 2014. I was just a baby Christian then, still finding my way in my newfound faith. As I mentioned earlier, I loved my horses. In a lot of ways, I took better care of them than I did myself. My favorite riding horse was Sweet Pea. She was nearly four years old at the time, and she and I had this unbelievable bond. All I had to do was move my legs a little bit or make certain noises and she'd respond. When you have a connection like that with a huge animal, I'm telling you, it is awesome. We jumped. We ran. We'd go up hills nobody else would mount. Real cowboys offered me good money for Sweet Pea. That was how good she was.

One day, I was out feeding my horses before work when Sweet Pea suddenly dropped to the ground with a thud. I rushed over to her, knowing that she had been losing weight over the past few months. I figured it was maybe from all the hard riding, though I had also noticed a decrease in her stamina. I comforted her, but I had to go to work. I called the veterinarian and met him out there a few hours later. Sweet Pea was still listless. Even worse, her gums had become bone white, not pink like they should've been.

I had been boarding several horses for other people, and I knew some hadn't wormed their animals like they should have. Sure enough, Sweet Pea had contracted unbelievable worms that were sucking the blood out of her. The vet also diagnosed her with a heart murmur. He told me she'd have to really be doctored up, giving me a daily regimen to follow with her. A week later, he returned, and Sweet Pea wasn't any better. He said the only thing that could be done for her at that point was a complete blood transfusion. That was no small task, and it came at no small cost, but there was no question whether or not I'd get it done. When I asked him about her chances of survival even with a successful transfusion, he said it was no better than fifty-fifty.

I made preparations to have her specially transported all the way to Auburn University, the only place in Alabama where such a procedure was possible. The night before I was scheduled to take her in, God spoke to me. I want to say it was in a dream, but it may not have been. Yet I can hear the voice as clear today as I did then.

He said, "Jeannie, believe in me."

I woke up, canceled the appointment, and I didn't take her in. I actually gave my precious Sweet Pea to God. It was a tremendous leap of faith.

Well, you can guess what happened. The vet returned two months later for his regular visit for all of my animals, and he saw one of my four horses standing tall and vibrant in the distance. "Which horse is that?" he asked.

"That's Sweet Pea!" I said.

"No."

"Yeah, it is!"

He shook his head. "I thought she was going to die that day."

I could've smacked him. "You didn't tell me that!"

"I know," he said. "I couldn't. She looks fantastic!"

It was a miracle. God just wanted to know if I was willing to have the faith to give my horse over to His care. In giving Sweet Pea to Him, He didn't take her away from me.

Personal reflection

1. Tell me all about your leap of faith that was directed by God?
2. If you haven't taken one, what is holding you back?
3. How do you go about trusting God? Explain.
4. How can you apply these responses to make sure you don't quit five minutes before the miracle happens?

Personal application

Step out in faith and bring glory to God, knowing 1) you can believe and trust Him, 2) doing so makes you more dependent upon Him, and 3) developing that dependence causes you to fully surrender to your loving Lord and His will for your life.

*   *   *

TEACHING POINT #12. GUARD YOUR HEART.

The psalmist cut no corners when he wrote, "I will not look with approval on anything that is vile. I hate what faithless people do; I will have no part in it." (Psalm 101:3) God wants us to protect our hearts from the things of this fallen world. We must watch what we take in, because the old adage is true: garbage in, garbage out. This includes music, television, movies, books, and, yes, even the people you let into your life.

It is so easy to fall into sin. David, who the Bible identifies as a man after God's own heart, often let his guard down. Perhaps the most notable occasion is recorded for us in 2 Samuel 11. As King of Israel, David sent Joab and the Israelite army out to battle while he stayed home. "One evening David got up from his bed and walked around on the roof of the palace. From the roof he saw a woman bathing. The woman was very beautiful, and David sent someone to find out about her. The man said, 'She is Bathsheba, the daughter of Eliam and the wife of Uriah the Hittite.' Then David sent messengers to get her. She came to him, and he slept with her. (Now she was purifying herself from her monthly uncleanness.) Then she went back home. The woman conceived and sent word to David, saying, 'I am pregnant.'" (2 Samuel 11:2-5)

David neither guarded his eyes nor his heart at a time he should've been at war alongside his men, and it cost him.

How did he respond? He tried to cover up his wrongdoing. "David sent this word to Joab: 'Send me Uriah the Hittite.' And Joab sent him to David. When Uriah came to him, David asked him how Joab was, how the soldiers were and how the war was going. Then David said to Uriah, 'Go down to your house and wash your feet.' So Uriah left the palace, and a gift from the king was sent after him. But Uriah slept at the entrance to the palace with all his master's servants and did not go down to his house. David was told, 'Uriah did not go home.' So he asked Uriah, 'Haven't you just come from a military campaign? Why didn't you go home?' Uriah said to David, 'The ark and Israel and Judah are staying in tents, and my commander Joab and my lord's men are camped in the open country. How could I go to my house to eat and drink and make love to my wife? As surely as you live, I will not do such a thing!' Then David said to him, 'Stay here one more day, and tomorrow I will send you back.' So Uriah remained in Jerusalem that day and the next. At David's invitation, he ate and drank with him, and David made him drunk. But in the evening Uriah went out to sleep on his mat among his master's servants; he did not go home." (2 Samuel 11:6-13)

Well, that didn't work—so what was there left for David to do? Recognize Uriah's honor, fess up to his affair, and take responsibility for the child Bathsheba was bearing?

Nope.

"In the morning David wrote a letter to Joab and sent it with Uriah. In it he wrote, 'Put Uriah out in front where the fighting is fiercest. Then withdraw from him so he will be struck down and die.' So while Joab had the city under siege, he put Uriah at a place where he knew the strongest defenders were. When the men of the city came out and fought against Joab, some of the men in David's army fell; moreover, Uriah the Hittite died." (2 Samuel 11:14-17)

I encourage you to read the rest of 2 Samuel chapters 11 and 12 for yourself. It's an incredible, poignant story of a man who didn't guard his heart and brought horrific consequences on himself and others as a result. It also shows how much David's God—our God—still loved him despite his poor decisions.

To guard our hearts, I totally believe in having a spiritual mentor. I prayed for God to give me direction on who my mentor should be, and He did. Mine is very much an accountability partner who will not hesitate to call me out on things she knows I shouldn't be seeing and doing. I give her that authority in my life. She helps protect me from deception, which is vital since we do not know when we are being deceived by the enemy. She speaks life into me as well. I encourage you to find a spiritual mentor, being sure to choose someone who is ahead of where you are spiritually and shares your commitment to Jesus.

Personal reflection

1. Knowing God instructs you to guard your heart, consider how you have taken your guard down. What led to it coming down? What can you do differently in the future to bolster the guarding of your heart?

2. What are your false idols—those things that cause you to let your guard down? They could be money, relationships, power, or just about anything else. List them.

3. For each false idol listed, what can you do to better guard your heart against them?

4. How can you apply these responses to make sure you

don't quit five minutes before the miracle happens?

Personal application

As you protect your heart from the things of this fallen world, remember that 1) sin is everywhere, 2) allowing it to slip into your life moves you away from the Lord, and 3) the thing God wants most from you is to be a person after His own heart.

*   *   *

TEACHING POINT #13. CHOOSE FORGIVENESS.

Sometimes, forgiveness is an OUCH! There have been times when I have not wanted to be obedient to God's directive to give forgiveness or ask for forgiveness from others, the latter being the hardest of all. However, I've discovered that forgiveness keeps me humble and soft-hearted. Forgiveness has cut my ties to the past, and that's something only God can do as we are willing to forgive. God will not force anything upon you. He might make you very uncomfortable, but He will not violate your own free will. There have been people in my past who I have found nearly impossible to forgive. Yet as He began to soften my heart, my prayers changed drastically over a period of time. Through this process, I started praying the same prayers for them that I was praying for myself. Praying for their families. Praying that if they were not saved, they, too, would make that turn toward Jesus. Through forgiveness, God continues to heal me.

The hardest person to forgive was me. The Lord had wiped the slate clean, but I would not forgive myself.

Hence, I actually put myself above God, making *me* higher than Him! That's the very height of pride, isn't it? Over time and with the help of therapy, though, I began to choose forgiveness for myself through the grace of God and His unconditional love. Now, I live every day in joy! There are definitely mornings that I wake up and do not feel joyful. But, just as I choose to be thankful, I also choose to have joy. It comes from knowing Jesus!

My favorite story from the Bible about choosing forgiveness is found in the book of Jonah. In it, we discover that Jonah was called by God to preach at Nineveh because of its great wickedness, but instead of obeying, he took a ship in the opposite direction. His disobedience arose from his fear that the Ninevites would heed his message and repent, and that God would forgive the city which had for many years oppressed his own land. "Then the Lord sent a great wind on the sea, and such a violent storm arose that the ship threatened to break up. All the sailors were afraid and each cried out to his own god. And they threw the cargo into the sea to lighten the ship. But Jonah had gone below deck, where he lay down and fell into a deep sleep. The captain went to him and said, 'How can you sleep? Get up and call on your god! Maybe he will take notice of us so that we will not perish.' Then the sailors said to each other, 'Come, let us cast lots to find out who is responsible for this calamity.' They cast lots and the lot fell on Jonah." (Jonah 1:4-7)

The crew, aware that Jonah was "running away from the Lord" (verse 10), became angry at him. "The sea was getting rougher and rougher. So they asked him, 'What should we do to you to make the sea calm down for us?' 'Pick me up and throw me into the sea,' he replied, 'and it will become calm. I know that it is my fault that this great storm has come upon you.'" (Jonah 1:11-12) Incredible! Eventually, the crew did just that—and you'll remember what happened next: the Lord provided a huge fish, it swallowed Jonah, and in it he stayed for three days and three nights. Within his submerged prison, Jonah did what any of us would do in the same situation—he prayed, and he decided to make good on his vow before God. "The Lord commanded the fish, and it vomited Jonah onto dry land." (Jonah 2:10)

But that only began Jonah's forgiveness journey. He went to Nineveh, preached exactly as God instructed, and the Ninevites indeed repented. "When God saw what they did and how they turned from their evil ways, he relented and did not bring on them the destruction he had threatened." (Jonah 3:10) But this did not please Jonah. Despite his obedience, Jonah still needed to learn about forgiveness—and the Lord taught him in a most unusual way.

"The Lord God provided a leafy plant and made it grow up over Jonah to give shade for his head to ease his discomfort, and Jonah was very happy about the plant. But at dawn the next day God provided a worm, which chewed the plant so that it withered. When the sun rose, God provided a scorching east wind, and the sun blazed on Jonah's head so that he grew faint. He wanted to die, and said, 'It would be better for me to die than to live.'"

"But God said to Jonah, 'Is it right for you to be angry about the plant?' 'It is,' he said. 'And I'm so angry I wish I were dead.'"

"But the Lord said, 'You have been concerned about this plant, though you did not tend it or make it grow. It sprang up overnight and died overnight. And should I not have concern for the great city of Nineveh, in which there are more than a hundred and twenty thousand people who cannot tell their right hand from their left—and also many animals?'" (Jonah 4:6-11)

Jonah didn't want to forgive, but the lesson ended up being about Jonah's own heart. He discovered the truth Paul later shared in Ephesians 4:32—a truth God wants us to live out every day with joy in our hearts. "Be kind and compassionate to one another, forgiving each other, just as in Christ God forgave you."

Personal reflection

1. What are you holding onto that needs your forgiveness?
2. When have you found it difficult to forgive yourself? Explain how this made you feel.
3. Make a list of all of the people who need your forgiveness in their lives, and begin praying for them daily. Among those prayers, ask God to continue to soften your heart toward them.
4. How can you apply these responses to make sure you don't quit five minutes before the miracle happens?

Personal application

Choose forgiveness today. 1) I challenge you for the next 30 days to pray for an individual who needs your forgiveness. He will lead you, and I promise you, your heart will change. 2) If God can forgive you for all you have done, you can forgive those who have wronged and hurt you. 3) God will lead you toward forgiveness as you ask Him to reveal any unforgiveness harbored in your heart. Know that this is more about your heart and your freedom than theirs.

*   *   *

TEACHING POINT #14. BE A LEADER!

I have always been a natural born leader but, oh boy, did I ever need to be refined by the Lord. Not only has God helped me to become a better leader, but I have learned what it means to lead people to Jesus! In Matthew 28:19-20, Jesus tells us, "Therefore go and make disciples of all nations, baptizing them in the name of the Father and of the Son and of the Holy Spirit, and teaching them to obey everything I have commanded you. And surely I am with you always, to the very end of the age." What a beautiful blessing this is—and serving others in this way has impacted my overall leadership skills in the very best way. It's been said that "if serving is beneath you, leadership is beyond you," and that is so true.

God prepared me to carry this mantle of leadership by teaching me how my actions must not cause another person to stumble. I have to be constantly aware of my words, my actions, and what message I am sending to others through both. As I lead, I will draw others to Christ. Today, God has blessed me even further by allowing me to become a mentor to others. The ladies I have mentored have taught me so much, and to have an opportunity to mentor them is such a gift. I am raw and authentic in my approach to mentoring, and I allow the Holy Spirit to guide me. To be most effective, I also read books on leadership and mentoring, becoming a seeker of wisdom. I pray to always be a seeker and to be on fire for Jesus!

Scripture gives us an incredible example of how to lead in the story of Moses. There are many accounts from his great life that speak to his leadership abilities, but the one I love the most shows his humility and meekness (two qualities that were longtime weaknesses for me). It's in

Exodus 18 and involves Moses and his father-in-law, Jethro. "Moses told his father-in-law about everything the Lord had done to Pharaoh and the Egyptians for Israel's sake and about all the hardships they had met along the way and how the Lord had saved them. Jethro was delighted to hear about all the good things the Lord had done for Israel in rescuing them from the hand of the Egyptians. He said, 'Praise be to the Lord, who rescued you from the hand of the Egyptians and of Pharaoh, and who rescued the people from the hand of the Egyptians. Now I know that the Lord is greater than all other gods, for he did this to those who had treated Israel arrogantly.'" (Exodus 18:8-11)

The next day, Moses went to work serving as a judge for the people of Israel, an all-day leadership task that was both essential and exhausting. "When his father-in-law saw all that Moses was doing for the people, he said, 'What is this you are doing for the people? Why do you alone sit as judge, while all these people stand around you from morning till evening?' Moses answered him, 'Because the people come to me to seek God's will. Whenever they have a dispute, it is brought to me, and I decide between the parties and inform them of God's decrees and instructions.'"

"Moses' father-in-law replied, 'What you are doing is not good. You and these people who come to you will only wear yourselves out. The work is too heavy for you; you cannot handle it alone. Listen now to me and I will give you some advice, and may God be with you. You must be the people's representative before God and bring their disputes to him. Teach them his decrees and instructions, and show them the way they are to live and how they are to behave. But select capable men from all the people—men who fear God, trustworthy men who hate dishonest gain—and appoint them as officials over thousands, hundreds, fifties and tens. Have them serve as judges for the people at all times, but have them bring every difficult case to you; the simple cases they can decide themselves. That will make your load lighter, because they will share it with you. If you do this and God so commands, you will be able to stand the strain, and all these people will go home satisfied.'"

"Moses listened to his father-in-law and did everything he said." (Exodus 18:14-24)

No wonder Deuteronomy 34:10 said that "no prophet has risen in Israel like Moses, whom the Lord knew face to face." As a leader, Moses knew when to listen and adapt.

Personal reflection

1. You may not feel like a leader, but you are. Identify three God-given traits you possess for leadership.
2. What do these traits tell you about *how* you can lead—and for *who?*
3. What stops you from leading? List them, along with how you can come against these obstacles.
4. How can you apply these responses to make sure you don't quit five minutes before the miracle happens?

Personal application

As you consider how you can lead others to God's glory, don't forget, 1) when God calls you to lead, He will provide you with the resources. 2) All of the leaders in the Bible had weaknesses. God often uses the least qualified and most unexpected individuals to lead. 3) Leading comes in many different forms. It could be modeling character for your children, teaching a small church group, or supporting people at your place of employment. It can be anything.

* * *

TEACHING POINT #15. STAY HUMBLE.

There is no way I cannot be humble when God has poured His grace and mercy upon me. When I look where He brought me from and how He saved me, that raw emotion brings me to tears of joy. I know for a fact the truth from Proverbs 11:2 that "when pride comes, then comes disgrace, but with humility comes wisdom."

Of course, true humility requires courage as well—the kind of courage where we do not care about what others think, but our focus is solely on God. Luke 7:37-48 provides the ideal example of this from the life of a remarkable woman.

"A woman in that town who lived a sinful life learned that Jesus was eating at the Pharisee's house, so she came there with an alabaster jar of perfume. As she stood behind him at his feet weeping, she began to wet his feet with her tears. Then she wiped them with her hair, kissed them and poured perfume on them. When the Pharisee who had invited him saw this, he said to himself, 'If this man were a prophet, he would know who is touching him and what kind of woman she is—that she is a sinner.'"

"Jesus answered him, 'Simon, I have something to tell you.' 'Tell me, teacher,' he said."

"'Two people owed money to a certain moneylender. One owed him five hundred denarii, and the other fifty. Neither of them had the money to pay him back, so he forgave the debts of both. Now which of them will love him more?' Simon replied, 'I suppose the one who had the bigger debt forgiven.' 'You have judged correctly,' Jesus said."

"Then he turned toward the woman and said to Simon, 'Do you see this woman? I came into your house. You did not give me any water for my feet, but she wet my feet with her tears and wiped them with her hair. You did not give me a kiss, but this woman, from the time I entered, has not stopped kissing my feet. You did not put oil on my head, but she has poured perfume on my feet. Therefore, I tell you, her many sins have been for-given—as her great love has shown. But whoever has been forgiven little loves little.'"

"Then Jesus said to her, 'Your sins are forgiven.'"

For the woman, humility, displayed by her loving con-centration on the Lord, brought redemption and grace. As you stay humble, you'll experience His deliverance as well.

Personal reflection

1. How do you practice humility?
2. Why is humility important to God?
3. What does the woman's story from Luke 7 teach you about walking in humility with the Lord?
4. How can you apply these responses to make sure you don't quit five minutes before the miracle happens?

Personal application

Stay humble before God and others, keeping in mind that 1) pride is your doing; humility is God's doing, 2) pride separates us from God, but humility draws us nearer to Him, and 3) seeing and knowing all God has done in my life and the lives of others is so humbling.

Ask others to share their testimony of God's love and grace with you.

*   *   *

TEACHING POINT #16. DO NOT QUIT!

Press into your faith and allow God's strength to carry you. Remember, you stand in a place of victory because of what Jesus did for you on the cross. The enemy will try and deceive you, but you *are* victorious! There are so many stories in the Bible of perseverance and fortitude. What have I noticed about all of them? When you have God and He is providing the resources, you can press in and be successful. Follow through until it is complete. When you have God, *nothing* else is needed!

In Scripture, Nehemiah was someone who definitely did not quit. An incredible biblical leader in his own right, Nehemiah was the cupbearer to King Artaxerxes in the citadel of Susa when he received a fateful visitor.

"Hanani, one of my brothers, came from Judah with some other men, and I questioned them about the Jewish remnant that had survived the exile, and also about Jerusalem. They said to me, 'Those who survived the exile and are back in the province are in great trouble and disgrace. The wall of Jerusalem is broken down, and its gates have been burned with fire.'"

"When I heard these things, I sat down and wept. For some days I mourned and fasted and prayed before the God of heaven. Then I said: 'Lord, the God of heaven, the great and awesome God, who keeps his covenant of love with those who love him and keep his commandments, let your ear be attentive and your eyes open to hear the prayer your servant is praying before you day and night for your servants, the people of Israel. I confess the sins we Israelites, including myself and my father's family, have committed against you. We have acted very wickedly toward you. We have not obeyed the commands, decrees and laws you gave your servant Moses. Remember the instruction you gave your servant Moses, saying, 'If you are unfaithful, I will scatter you among the nations, but if you return to me and obey my commands, then even if your exiled people are at the farthest horizon, I will gather them from there and bring them to the place I have chosen as a dwelling for my Name.' They are your servants and your people, whom you redeemed by your great strength and your mighty hand. Lord, let your ear be attentive to the prayer of this your servant and to the prayer of your servants who delight in revering your name. Give your servant success today by granting him favor in the presence of this man." (Nehemiah 1:2-11)

From there, Nehemiah received the favor that he prayed for from the king and was able to go to Jerusalem to inspect the shattered walls of the city. He oversaw a strategy to use half the people for building while the other half kept watch for the Samaritans who threatened to attack. He overcame internal turmoil as well as opposition from outsiders (Nehemiah 4-7). Still, in the face of incredible stress and discouragement, Nehemiah brought order and safety to the people all while helping them focus on God, His teachings, and His purposes for them. "Then Nehemiah the governor, Ezra the priest and teacher of the Law, and the Levites who were instructing the people said to them all, 'This day is holy to the Lord your God. Do not mourn or weep.' For all the people had been weeping as they listened to the words of the Law. Nehemiah said,

'Go and enjoy choice food and sweet drinks, and send some to those who have nothing prepared. This day is holy to our Lord. Do not grieve, for the joy of the Lord is your strength.'" (Nehemiah 8:9-10)

Personal reflection

1. What does the enemy use against you in an attempt to get you to quit? Recognize this as condemnation.
2. When you have quit, how did you feel about yourself? Explain.
3. When you did not quit and pressed in, how did you feel about yourself? Explain.
4. How can you apply these responses to make sure you don't quit five minutes before the miracle happens?

Personal application

Remember, 1) when that first thought comes into your mind telling you to quit, you still have so much more left in you. Find that last 10 percent. 2) God will give you exactly what you need to finish strong! 3) Be a Nehemiah, strong and confident in the Lord, and push forward. When God is with you, it doesn't make any difference who or what is against you!

NOTES

1   "I am accepted..." "I am secure..." and "I am significant..." statements are from Freedom in Christ Ministries. https://ficm.org/about-us/who-i-am-in-christ/

2   "What is the truth?" list is from Freedom in Christ Ministries' free downloads. https://ficm.org/wp-content/uploads/2013/04/What-is-the-Truth1.pdf

Conclusion

Turn Toward Jesus

"I have fought the good fight, I have finished the race, I have kept the faith."

2 Timothy 4:7

Through the process of writing this book, I have fallen deeper in love with God. When I did not want to be as raw and transparent as He wanted me to be, He ever so gently whispered or nudged me into His will. I knew what He wanted of me, and my heart's desire was to totally surrender to Him. Yes, there were times I experienced emotional pain as God cut away the dead and brought forth the new. Was it worth it, you ask? Hands down, without hesitation, a resounding YES! Being in God's will is the very best high I have ever experienced! The healing that has taken place in my heart has been nothing less than profound. God took this crushed-in-spirit sinner and made me more like Christ. I am still a sinner, but I am not where I once was. I exude with joy in the Lord. My life is not without problems, but those problems do not own me. I keep hanging out—for five minutes, five days, or five years, whatever it takes—waiting for the next miracle to happen.

The purpose of this book was, and is, for *you* to turn toward Jesus and deepen your relationship with Him. The very best decision I ever made was accepting Jesus Christ as my Lord and Savior, repenting for all of my sins, and asking for His forgiveness. So, I will leave you with the Salvation Prayer. Saying this prayer out loud with a humble heart will change *your* life forever!

Your sister in Christ, Jeannie

Father, it is written in your Word that if I confess with my mouth that Jesus is Lord and believe in my heart that you have raised Him from the dead, I shall be saved. Therefore, Father, I confess that Jesus is my Lord. I make Him Lord of my life right now. I believe in my heart that you raised Jesus from the dead. I renounce my past life with Satan and close the door to any of his devices. I thank you for forgiving me of all my sins. Jesus is my Lord and Savior, and I am a new creation. Old things have passed away; now, all things become new. In Jesus' name. Amen.

My baby Christening, 1958 in Washington, D.C., with my Godparents.

Me and my family, 1959 in Takoma Park, MD. Mom and dad, with Lois Jean on the top left, and Mary Virginia next to her.

As a baby with Mary Virginia, 1959. You can see the mischief in my smile.

Infant innocence, 1959.

My Fav! Cutting grass with Mom in Bethesda, MD. My stroller sure did the job!

In kindergarten, four years old, in 1962. Go Curious George!

My first Holy Communion in second grade, 1965.

That's me in the frilly collar and sleeves with my nephews and niece, Bethesda, MD, 1967.

Christmas 1977 after Mary Virginia's suicide attempt, Sanford, NC. Joyce, Mary Virginia's oldest daughter and my only niece, is at the bottom left. Also pictured here are Mary Virginia; me and my beloved Winkie; Willie, Mary Virginia's middle child; and my parents.

At a keg party where I shot dope, Louisburg, NC.

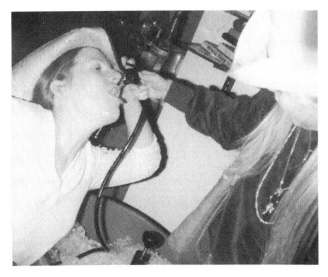

Who needs a glass? At a kegger in Raleigh, NC, 1979.

With my parents as a bridesmaid for a friend, six months after my sexual assault, Sanford, NC.

Hanging out with the bar softball team, Sarasota,
FL, 1981.

Just off the beach during another day of drinking,
Bradenton, FL, 1981.

After my abortion, Mary Virginia's suicide, and the start of my first lesbian relationship.

Tripping on Acid in Raleigh, NC.

Campbell University. Fall semester 1986, Buies Creek, NC.

Starting another night of partying. Spring 1987.

My undergraduate graduation picture, May 1987. I missed the graduation itself because of a drunken binge.

Patrolling third base for my bar softball team, Dunn, NC, 1987.

Masking my pain. Summer 1987.

During a black out. Summer 1987.

The morning after. Summer 1987.

Rafting on the rapids on the Nantahala River. I'm in the back, and it's right before I got tossed six feet into the air.

A medical record photo of my intake, July 1992 in Roanoke, AL. I was 19 months sober.

A medical record photo 30 days later of my discharge, August 1992, Roanoke, AL.

My undergraduate graduation at Campbell University,
Buies Creek, NC, May 1993.

Starting my master's program and moving to Alabama in
Fall 1993. I was almost three years sober.

In graduate school, May 1995

Graduation Day with my master's degree. Spring 1995, Carrollton, GA.

At the graduation party with friends. Spring 1995.

Tears of joy at my baptism, January 2014.

At the Easter Service, April 2014.

Goofing around as co-lead of the Sprouts small group.
Winter 2017.

Standing high and tall with friends at ECLI Graduation, May 2017.

The retreat in Mentone, AL where I received the call from Donna Sparks.

Silliness with the Sprouts small group, Christmas 2018.

Believe, staff and volunteers, October 2019. The inaugural No Limits Women's Retreat in Shocco Springs, AL.

Humbling myself before Him, No Limits Women's Retreat.

Anything is possible with God, No Limits Women's Retreat.

*The tree for the attendees to "leaf" behind their obstacles,
No Limits Women's Retreat.*

Praise and worship at the No Limits Women's Retreat.

Overseeing God's Creation, October 2020.

Pure JOY! October 2020.

Lines tangled, but no fear. Only God! October 2020.

God's goodness with Sweat Pea. Fall 2020.

Everyone wants some screen time! Fall 2020.

Living life to the fullest. Fall 2020.

Made in the USA
Columbia, SC
10 July 2021